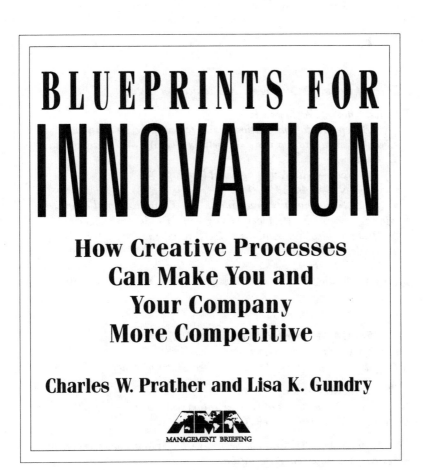

BLUEPRINTS FOR
INNOVATION

How Creative Processes Can Make You and Your Company More Competitive

Charles W. Prather and Lisa K. Gundry

AMA
MANAGEMENT BRIEFING

AMA Management Briefing

AMA MEMBERSHIP PUBLICATIONS DIVISION
AMERICAN MANAGEMENT ASSOCIATION

For information on how to order additional copies of this publication, see page 95.

Library of Congress Cataloging-in-Publication Data

Prather, Charles Wayne, 1941–
     Blueprints for innovation: how creative processes can make you
and your organization more competitive / Charles W. Prather and Lisa
K. Gundry.
          p.   cm.—(AMA management briefing)
          ISBN 0-8144-2359-0
          1. Creative ability in business.   2. Organizational change—
Management.   3. Problem solving.   4. Product management.
5. Technological innovations.   I. Gundry, Lisa K., 1958–   .
II. Title. III. Series.
HD53.P73   1995
658.4'03—dc20   *95-42760*
                                                                              CIP

© 1995 AMA Membership Publications Division
American Management Association, New York.
All rights reserved. Printed in the United States of America.

Bottom Line Innovation™
Is a registered trademark of C. W. Prather and Associates, 9 Yorkridge Trail,
Suite 106, Hockessin, DE 19707

This Management Briefing has been distributed to all members enrolled in the
American Management Association.

10   9   8   7   6   5   4   3   2   1

To **Pat, Juliannne,** and **Houston,** whose love sustains me.

—**Charles W. Prather**

To **Peter, Dylan,** and **Austin,** who daily enact the creative spirit and joy of discovery.

—**Lisa K. Gundry**

Contents

Acknowledgments

This book itself is a product of creativity—influenced by those with whom we have worked and by whom we have been taught. Our deepest gratitude is felt for Don Bohl, editor, American Management Association, who encouraged us to shape our thoughts and write this book. His belief in the power and the value of creative thinking and performance spurred us on towards this goal.

Charles W. Prather:

Dr. David Tanner's inspiration and personal interest opened the doors to the world of creativity and innovation for me, as he has done for countless others. Without his dedication to creativity, and without his personal interest in me, this book would have never been written.

My Mother's inspiration and rejoicing at my achievements is especially acknowledged.

Lastly, the many people who have contributed their time and stories to enrich this book deserve special thanks.

Lisa K. Gundry:

Jill Kickul, one of the most creative persons I've met, deserves thanks, as do David Drehmer and Ray Coye of DePaul University who first unveiled all the possibilities of creativity applied to organizational behavior. Heartfelt appreciation goes to Denise Rousseau, of Carnegie Mellon University, whose interest in work cultures stimulated my own. Finally, my parents, husband, and sons have been a wellspring of support (and creativity) in my attempt to combine imagination and organization professionally and personally.

Introduction:

Why *You* Should Read This Book

You have picked up this book because you want to become more innovative, and you want your organization (or team) to become more innovative as well. You know that creativity and innovation will be the keys to effectiveness and competitive strength in the 21st Century. Rest assured—this book will help you reach your goal.

As you read the following chapters, you will discover that problem solving lies at the center of *every* job in your organization, and that creativity lies at the heart of problem solving. In this way, all employees in your company are paid to be creative. By institutionalizing creativity, you and your organization will go a long way toward increasing employees' problem-solving abilities.

You should read this book because you will learn of success stories that you can put to good use in your own firm. You will develop ideas you may otherwise have never had—ideas that can ultimately contribute to your bottom line. When you put into practice the principles described in this book, you will become a better leader. People in your organization (or on your team) will follow your lead as you help them solve tough problems in new and unexpected ways.

You will also discover that customers and suppliers can contribute many valuable ideas and suggestions. Of course, the concept of listening to the input of customers and suppliers is not new; however, you will likely find that inviting major customers to your creative problem-solving sessions can put you ahead in your field, and increase customer loyalty as well.

You will learn that people prefer different problem-solving styles. Truly valuing (instead of just tolerating) those who prefer a style different from your own is difficult, but a giant step toward improving innovation where you work.

We assume that you already hold a leadership position in your firm. You have probably attained this position because you think about your work and your organization in new and unusual ways, and you accomplish your objectives inventively. But while your vision and knowledge have been essential to your current success, they cannot take you to even greater lengths until the others with whom you work are also equipped with the principles and mindset to carry out your vision. We have seen companies with strong and passionate leaders struggle and ultimately fail because they never gave their employees the tools to make the organization's vision a reality.

This book will provide you with the techniques you need to make creativity and innovation an everyday process, which will help you attain your vision and reach new organizational milestones. It will enable you to adopt a new, innovative style of management. And this new management style will help you bring out the creative potential that is likely lying dormant within the halls of your office or plant.

1

The Innovative Organization

What do you do for yourself and for your organization? Undoubtedly, your work and professional activities include identifying and solving problems. Now, how would you describe the future of your organization? Uncertain? Competitive? Drastically different from the way it was ten years ago—or even just a few short months ago?

To remain healthy and profitable in the uncertain and competitive global business environment of the year 2000 and beyond, organizations *are finding that they must* address problems using new and unconventional approaches. As a result, companies are demanding that *employees* think about organizational problems and business issues in new and unconventional ways.

Today's senior managers are grappling with a host of complex issues. These include:

- What new products and services can we design, produce, distribute, or sell?
- How can we find ways to provide added value?
- How can we position our products, services, and processes so they stand out from our competitors'?

- How well are we serving our current markets, and how can we improve?
- What markets could we serve that we are currently not serving?

To answer these questions, organizations are seeking to apply creativity to problems and opportunities. They need to invent new ways of developing, producing, and distributing goods, services, and information. And they need employees who can help them move forward. As a result, the competencies and behaviors that are now becoming essential to competitiveness and effectiveness center on the creative process: Individuals who want to be successful must learn how to break with tradition, how to develop ideas and, eventually, how to do things in a new way.

The term *creativity*, which we use extensively throughout this book, has many connotations as it applies to business. Researchers, instructors, and consultants define it by referring to a variety of factors, including *attributes* (individuals' characteristics, such as independence, risk-taking, and intuitiveness); *conceptual skills* (the ability to organize and interpret information in pattern-breaking ways); *behaviors* (actions that produce inventions, innovations, and unexpected outcomes); and *processes* (the combination of individual talents, skills, and actions within an innovation-supporting organizational culture).

In this book, we distinguish "creativity" from "innovation" by using the former to refer to all activities that involve the generation of ideas. Innovation, on the other hand, refers to the implementation of viable business ideas generated as a result of the organization's creativity-supporting culture and structures.

THE "THREE ARENAS" MODEL

Based on close observation at the DuPont Center for Creativity and Innovation during its formative months in early 1991, we've identified three arenas that, as a group, tend to be present in all creative and innovative organizations (see Figure 1–1). Leaders who want their organization to become more creative and innovative will want to ensure that appropriate activities in each of these arenas occur.

One critical arena is *applications,* and it is in this arena that *bottom-line innovation* occurs. Bottom Line Innovation is a set of techniques and processes that generate new, useful, and unexpected solutions to important business problems. By focusing on the applications arena, an organization ensures that the "right" problems are identified, that unexpected ideas are generated and the most effective ideas selected, and that

Figure 1–1. The three arenas of the innovative organization.

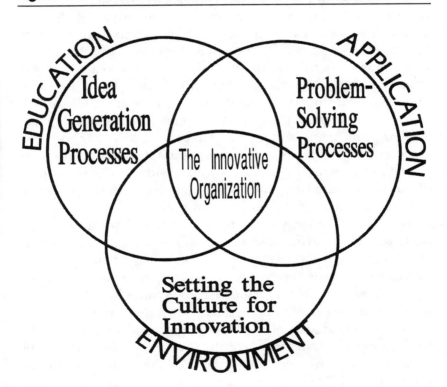

sponsorship and action plans are developed. This arena is discussed more completely in Chapter 3.

Another arena is *education*. Specifically, we mean the process of teaching people the basic concepts of creativity, and demonstrating to them specific tools for "thinking out of the box"—for moving beyond brainstorming. An organization's essential task in this arena is to enable people at all levels to develop new, useful, and unexpected ideas. This arena is discussed in more detail in Chapter 4.

The third arena is *setting the climate for innovation*. The climate (worker's perceptions of what it's like to work here) is a critical part of the innovative organization. Unfortunately, it is also one that leaders often neglect, most likely because the climate is seldom perfect, and exposed imperfections could be viewed as a leadership problem. Nine dimensions of the creative and innovative climate have been identified (Isaksen, et al. 1994), and we describe a quantitative method for measuring these nine dimensions, so that when leaders want to make improvements, they know where to target. The subject of organizational climate is treated more completely in Chapter 5.

Let's take a quick preview of the remaining three chapters.

Managers who want to encourage employees to become more creative and innovative must take into account the preferred problem-solving style of each individual. Whenever people solve problems, they are being creative, so the appropriate question becomes not "How creative *are* you?" but "*How* are you creative?" An individual's preferred style determines which parts of the creativity and innovation process he or she will enjoy most, and which parts he or she is most suited to. Managers who understand the concept of problem-solving style will be best able to assemble powerful teams. We discuss problem-solving style in more detail in Chapter 6.

The configuration of individuals, groups, and responsibilities within an organization can have a strong influence on its creative and innovative capabilities. For this reason, we've devoted Chapter 7 to the role of organizational structure. To help with this discussion, we present examples of structures that enable, or disable, innovation.

Finally, in Chapter 8 we will discuss your own journey toward creativity and innovation. It is a journey without end, but with plenty of significant milestones and successes along the way.

2

Innovation 101: The Basics

Creativity and innovation, at their simplest, are forms of problem solving—but they are very specific forms. When we refer to problem solving in this book, keep in mind that we are *not* referring to the useful and familiar Kepner-Trego style of logic-based analysis, which seeks to return systems to normalcy after some deviation has occurred. Instead, we are talking about problem solving that enables us to achieve a new, higher level of performance.

To clarify this point, assume that you own a broken television. Using the former type of problem solving—a process of logical elimination—the skilled technician will identify the cause of the problem, and fix the unit so that it returns to its previous, unbroken state. Now assume, by contrast, that you have a working television, but want to enhance its performance. Using the latter type of problem solving, you may create a way for it to display a 3-D picture, or a picture with improved sound capabilities.

As Figure 2–1 shows, we see creativity and innovation working together to form a specific problem-solving process.

Figure 2–1. The innovative problem-solving model.

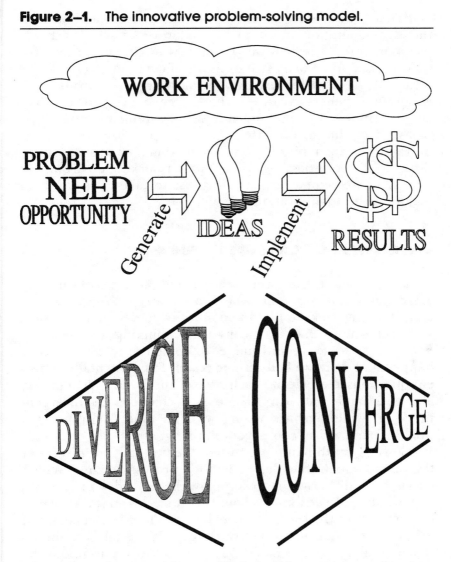

The process begins with a problem, need, or opportunity, then proceeds through idea generation (the center of the model) and implementation, and ultimately yields a result. Hovering over the model is a cloud labeled "Work Environment."

What kind of effect does the working environment have on the idea-generation and implementation processes? It actually has many effects, which we will discuss in Chapter 5, but for now, let's examine one as an example. Take a closer look at the center of the model in Figure 2–1. Most organizations have an easier time being "creative"—that is, generating ideas—than being "innovative"—that is, successfully implementing those ideas. Often the reason is that people are paralyzed by the fear of failure, which makes trying something new exceedingly difficult, if not impossible. In this way, a working environment that promotes employee unwillingness to take risks can be a major barrier to innovation.

DIVERGENT AND CONVERGENT THINKING

Notice that near the bottom of the model, two types of thinking are displayed: *divergent thinking* and *convergent thinking*. Divergent thinking seeks to build and amplify, to decorate, to make something more than it is; convergent thinking, on the other hand, seeks to select and judge, to compare, to make things happen and deliver a bottom-line result. Fundamentally different questions characterize each style of thinking: "What's good about it?" and "How can it be used?" characterizes divergent thinking, while "What's wrong with it?" and "Why won't it work?" characterizes convergent thinking.

Convergent thinking used when the task calls for divergent thinking dampens the idea-generation process. Asking "What's wrong with it?" leads us to compare the new idea or thought with what we already know about that subject, and if the former doesn't fit with the latter, we label it "a bad idea" (particularly if we did not come up with it ourselves). We've all been in so-called "brainstorming" meetings where someone summons the courage to suggest an approach to solving a problem, only to have it quashed by another individual, who uses a killer phrase such as, "It won't work," "The boss won't go for it," or "It's not in the budget." These killer phrases are a sure tip-off that someone is thinking convergently—asking the question, "What's wrong with it?"

In our experience, it is the experts—those individuals with great knowledge, experience, and credibility—who are the very first to tell everyone why a new idea will not work. However, it is precisely these experts who have the most to contribute when it comes to innovation! In our workshops, we teach participants to throw paper balls at other participants who judge an idea prematurely. It's a lighthearted way of making a very serious point: It's essential to use divergent thinking when the task is to generate ideas, and convergent thinking when the task is to begin implementation.

THE FIVE PITFALLS THAT HINDER INNOVATION

Below are five major pitfalls people and organizations tend to fall into when trying to become more innovative. As you read, see how many of these apply to you or your organization, so that you can sidestep them at every upcoming opportunity.

1. Identifying the Wrong Problem

You may have wondered why problems often don't stay solved, or solutions never quite work out as expected, despite your best efforts. Many times it's because the wrong problem was defined. For example, consider the case of a large synthetic-fiber producer. The company's management originally sponsored a workshop to help find ways to reduce the manufacturing cost of a particular product—but instead, the participants developed a highly successful way to increase the sales of a profitable segment of that product line. How were they able to change their focus in this way? They simply examined the problem within the broader context of profitability, and discovered that the *real* problem was low profits.

2. Judging Ideas too Quickly

We've already discussed how adults tend toward convergent thinking when the task calls for individuals to be divergent.

This tendency always leads people to judge ideas too quickly, thereby effectively squelching the creative process. All employees (but especially, the experts) need to understand the distinction between divergent and convergent thinking, and need to learn to put their tendency to converge "on hold" at certain times, to allow new ideas to flourish. Children are naturally divergent in their thinking because they don't yet have a great storehouse of knowledge and experience against which to judge new ideas. We must learn to become more "child-like" by putting our strong tendency to converge "on hold" for a little while, asking, as children do, "What's right about this idea?"

3. Stopping with the First Good Idea

The first good idea is *never* the best. That's because it was the easiest to come up with, so there's little doubt that competitors have already thought of it, too. Also, the first idea is generally derived from brainstorming—and brainstorming, effective as it is, isn't set up to change thinking patterns. Most often during a brainstorming session, the "usual ideas" emerge. Perhaps they are slightly rearranged, but they are almost never the truly unexpected ideas that are needed to surpass the competition. By contrast, the very best ideas—the ones most often chosen to be implemented—are two to three times more likely to come from thoughts that occur after the ability to generate ideas via brainstorming has been exhausted.

4. Failing to "Get the Bandits on the Train"

Imagine you are on a train in the American West in the late 1800s. Your train is traveling from Laramie to Tombstone, Wyoming, and you fear that bandits will come from behind tall rocks and dynamite the track. How can you keep that from happening?

One answer is to "get the bandits on the train." In an organizational sense, this means figuring out whose support you must have or who could derail your project, and finding a way to get them on the train—to have them become part of the project early on. At DuPont's Center for Creativity and Innovation, leaders confirmed that when a manager (or managers) with the authority to commit dollars and personnel actively participates throughout the problem-solving process (from problem definition through idea generation and action planning), he or she does not "dynamite the track."

5. Obeying Rules That Don't Exist

There's a Gary Larsen cartoon that shows two cowboys crouched behind their covered wagons as flaming arrows head their way. One says to the other, "Hey, they're lighting their arrows! Can they do that?"

Many times we hamstring ourselves by assuming we cannot do something, when in fact there is no reason why we can't. We may assume that a rule must be obeyed when actually there is no such rule at all. For example, have you ever assumed that you had to do all the work assigned you? Or that you had to do everything anyone asked? Of course you have. Examining our set of assumptions, and then reversing them, is one easy method of generating new ideas.

Now that we've examined the pitfalls of innovation, we can turn our attention to the tools and techniques that will improve our problem-solving capabilities.

3

Tools and Techniques for Problem Solving

In an organizational setting, the purpose of creativity is to solve problems. Groups and teams (as opposed to individuals) are especially good at being creative and, by extension, at solving problems, because of the effects of synergy. Certain techniques and processes, however, can make groups and teams even better problem solvers, by helping them enhance their creative abilities. We call this collection of techniques and processes *Bottom Line Innovation.*

ASSIGNING AN EFFECTIVE FACILITATOR

Every problem-solving group or team needs someone with meeting-process knowledge and facilitation skills to run its meetings. The facilitator can be an external consultant or someone from within the organization, but not a participant on the team; otherwise, he or she might be tempted to get too involved in the content of the meeting, and lose sight of the process. The facilitator directs the team's energy to purposeful action, which can greatly magnify its productivity. Without a facilitator, team members may end up working against one another, rather than all for the good of the organization.

ADOPTING PARALLEL PROCESSING

Serial processing occurs when the facilitator becomes the channel through which all information must pass, standing at the flip chart and recording ideas as group members call them out. This is the least effective way to run a meeting, because the process can go only as fast as the facilitator can write, which is a lot slower than the group can generate ideas.

A better approach is *parallel processing,* whereby participants capture their own ideas using "Post-It" notes. Each group member writes down his or her ideas, one idea per Post-It note; then the members take turns reading their ideas aloud and placing their Post-It notes on the flip chart. This process guarantees that the most ideas possible are considered, that both timid and gregarious members contribute, and that all members recognize that the group is hearing and considering their ideas.

Parallel processing can be used during any step of the problem-solving process outlined below, from defining the right problem to choosing an idea to implement.

DEFINING THE RIGHT PROBLEM

People solve only the problems they define. If they define the wrong one, they will often solve it in an excellent manner, then wonder why the solution never worked well. DuPont's Center for Creativity and Innovation helped business units solve problems in unusual and unexpected ways. In all of the problem-solving sessions that were run, the Center's staff found that *not one unit* had identified its problem accurately before the session.

Defining the right problem will consume several hours of

intense group time, as the group conducts divergent thinking to come up with various potential problem statements, then zeroes in on the one to be solved. Of all the tasks involved in problem solving, this one is the most important, because it determines the subject matter on which employees will focus their attention to generate ideas.

The wording of the problem statement is critical. The three guidelines for writing problem statements are:

• Always begin with "How might we . . . " (or "How might I . . .")

• Never suggest a solution. (For example, you would never write, "How might we improve safety by more training?")

• Include only one problem. (For example, you would never write, "How might we increase the quality and reduce the cost of making our product?")

How can group members be sure that they are defining the right problem? A good approach is for members to envision an ideal future state, then back up and determine what problems would need to be solved to help the group arrive there. This method is diagrammed in Figure 3–1. Specifically, each participant, again using "Post-It" notes, should complete the following phrase at least 10 times: "Wouldn't it be nice if . . ." Members then group the notes according to subject matter, title each grouping appropriately, and develop a possible problem statement for each grouping. The major themes of the individual notes making up the grouping need to be embodied in the problem statement.

For example, assume that the team develops a grouping entitled "Communication." The problem statement stemming from this group might read, "How might we improve communication among organizational units?" Following this step, the team would work on the remaining groupings, then priortize all the problem statements it had developed.

To demonstrate how effective this method can be, consider the actual case of a problem-solving team at a Midwestern

Figure 3–1. Define the right problems.

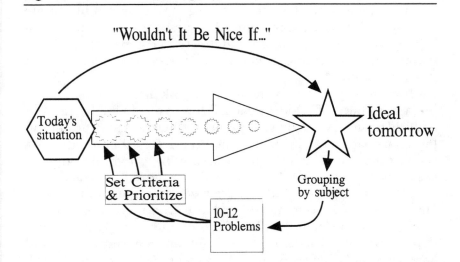

research institute. The team initially believed its challenge was, "How can we convince our clients to participate in designing our programs so we can be of more value to them?" However, members soon realized that this statement was defective, because it contained the elements of a solution. When they conducted the process described above, they realized that their true challenge was to *increase the value* of their services. Consequently, the group developed two new problem statements, each of which would have to be addressed separately: "How might we improve the benefits to our customers of the work we do?" and "How might we reduce the costs of delivering these benefits?" The group ultimately realized that if it had stuck with its initial statement, and tried to encourage customers to participate in designing programs, the problem of increasing value would not have been addressed.

"SQUEEZING OUT" THE IDEAS THROUGH BRAINSTORMING

When individuals participate in a problem-solving workshop, they are generally familiar with the problem area, and they come to the workshop with their own information, prejudices, and ideas, many of which may have been rattling around inside their heads for quite some time. The first step of any problem-solving workshop, then, should be to recognize these ideas through brainstorming, using the parallel-processing approach described above.

It's a good idea for the facilitator to ask members to contribute a minimum of 10 ideas each. They can usually do this, but with difficulty. After these have been discussed and posted on flip-chart paper, the facilitator should ask for 10 more ideas—a request that will usually be met with audible groans, as employees think to themselves, "There *aren't* any more." The facilitator must continue to push until there *really* aren't any more ideas. He or she can encourage the group with a metaphor, such as "We are digging in a gold field for gold nuggets." Eventually—that is, when participants have been pushed very hard, and have generated between 10 and 15 ideas each—the group will reach bedrock: Their minds have been drained, and they have no more to offer.

At this point, it's appropriate for the facilitator to talk about *tools and techniques for pattern-breaking* thinking. We will cover these tools in Chapter 4, but for now, we want to make the point that people will apply these tools only after their brainstorming ideas have been exhausted. People will not go outside their "thinking box" in search of new ideas until they have emptied their box of the kind of ideas they normally have.

We call this "emptying" process *brainstorming to exhaustion.* To illustrate how valuable it is, consider the case of an inexperienced facilitator running a workshop in Geneva, Switzerland. Without knowing better, the facilitator launched into pattern-breaking thinking without first conducting a brainstorming session. The "normal" ideas that would have surfaced during traditional brainstorming began appearing under the guise of pattern-breaking thinking. During the morning break, one participant said to the facilitator, "Sir, you are wasting your time and our money. We have gotten nothing from this that we couldn't have gotten by 'just thinking.' " Naturally the facilitator was miffed, but eventually he realized that the participant's words were a piece of golden advice. The participant helped the facilitator understand that groups must "brainstorm to exhaustion" *before starting* pattern-breaking thinking.

DECIDING WHICH IDEAS TO IMPLEMENT

Brainstorming generates many ideas, which enter what we call the "idea pool." Pattern-breaking thinking adds further to the pool. A group of 14 participants, for example, is likely to generate more than 500 ideas during several hours of work. With this many ideas, how is it possible to decide which ideas to implement?

Idea selection and implementation make up the convergence phase of the problem-solving process. The facilitator can encourage participants to view this process as a kind of group shopping expedition: Group members should imagine they are all in a grocery store with one shopping cart to share, and together they must pick the best ideas from the idea pool and put them in the cart for further refinement. They should select 10 to 20 percent of the total number of ideas, based only on the criterion, "If we could do this, it would really contribute to solving the problem at hand." If there were 500 ideas in the idea pool, we would want to select 10–20 percent, or about 50 ideas from the pool. Assuming seven participants, each one gets to select seven ideas that have not been selected by another participant. The ideas are written on duplicate "Post-It" notes so as not to disrupt the original idea pool by removing ideas from it.

When the selections have been made, participants one by one physically place each idea on the idea grid shown in Figure 3–2 (the facilitator has previously prepared the idea grid and taped it to a large wall surface). As Figure 3–2 shows, the two dimensions of the idea grid are: Our Capability (to implement the idea), and its Potential (to solve the problem). The participant suggests which quadrant he or she believes the idea

Figure 3–2. The idea grid for selecting the best ideas.

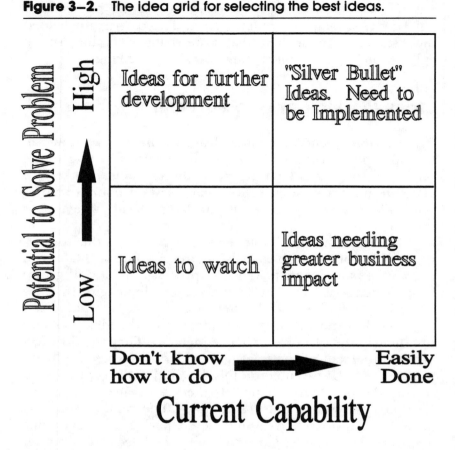

belongs on the idea grid, and with group discussion decides the best location.

When every participant has placed all their ideas on the grid, it will have four types of ideas. Those in the upper right quadrant (the "Silver Bullet" ideas) should be implemented right away, since they are likely to be successful, and group members have the know-how to enact them; those in the upper left quadrant need additional development (if they involve technical matters, R&D programs can be drawn from this quadrant); the ideas in the lower right quadrant need to be reworked so they will demonstrate greater potential for success (an appropriate business unit can usually help with this task); and finally, those in the lower left quadrant are best left alone for now, since their value is questionable, and the group lacks the ability to implement them (they may become viable, however, if business conditions or group skills change).

This process of group discussion during idea placement on the grid is immensely valuable. For example, in a workshop with a major oil company, one participant was about to place an idea in the upper left quadrant, meaning that it had great potential, but to do it was an "unknown." Instantly another participant called out, "I know how to do that!" The discussion that followed enlightened the whole group, and the idea was moved to the upper right "Silver Bullet" quadrant so that implementation could begin.

Following this classification process, the group should focus on the upper right quadrant. Each participant should vote for the one idea that he or she believes would be most effective in solving the problem. Usually a clear winner will emerge, and that will be the first idea to be implemented. At that point, it's time for the group to improve its chances of implementation success.

IMPROVING YOUR BATTING AVERAGE BEFORE PICKING UP THE BAT

To help assure success in implementing the chosen idea, group members will want to develop a more complete picture of what implementation will require, by examining both the major components and the details of the solution. They can do this by constructing the tree diagram shown in Figure 3–3. Usually this exercise will be given to the implementation team. However, if time permits, the problem-solving team might well proceed and provide the output as recommendations to the implementation team.

Using a flip chart, the facilitator should write the selected

Figure 3–3. The tree diagram to strengthen ideas.

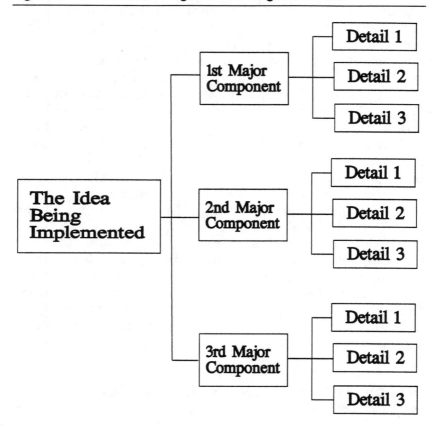

idea in the left hand square. Following the group's discussion, or combining the output from participants who have been working in groups of two or three, the facilitator should list each of the components that go into implementing that idea on the next level, and each detail required to accomplish each component on the level after that. This process should be continued until group members can conceive of no more details. To test the completeness of the tree diagram, have participants start at the right-most end, and working toward the left, ask themselves if they accomplish all the elements at each level, would the next highest level item be sure to happen. If any answer is "no," then some crucial item is missing at the level being considered, and participants should decide what must be done, and add the item. When this process is completed, members can be pretty certain that their implementation process has been fully analyzed, and no critical aspects have been overlooked.

In this chapter we have described *Bottom Line Innovation*, the set of techniques and processes that will help (1) ensure you have identified the right problem, (2) generate ideas, (3) select the best idea to implement, and (4) improve the idea before beginning implementation. In the next chapter, we will examine some tools and techniques to help generate ideas that go beyond brainstorming.

4

Tools and Techniques to Move Beyond Brainstorming

The term *brainstorming* was coined in 1953 by author Alex Osborn, an advertising executive who became passionately interested in the subject of creativity. In his book, *Applied Imagination,* he used "brainstorming" to refer to a process to help people develop new ideas. It principally refers to a session of any length during which a group of individuals uses only divergent thinking. The general rules for a brainstorming session are that individuals should (1) strive to come up with as many ideas as possible, (2) defer judgment of any idea, and (3) build upon the ideas of others.

Brainstorming is a beneficial technique, in that it has helped several generations of businesspeople develop more and better ideas than they otherwise might have. However, it does have its limitations. Essentially, brainstorming draws out from us ideas and concepts that already are within us (although they may emerge in new combinations or arrangements). It does *not* break our thinking patterns, which would allow us to think up truly unexpected ideas.

Take a look at Figure 4–1, which illustrates how people generally are prisoners locked inside their thinking boxes, the walls of which are formed by their logic and unstated assumptions. It is these thinking patterns that prevent us from generating truly unexpected ideas—the kind of ideas that can transform a business, and lead competitors to ask, "Why didn't we think of that?" To come up with unexpected ideas, we need a set of tools that we can use whenever we need, to help us

Figure 4–1. The walls of our "thinking box" are made of our unstated assumptions and logic.

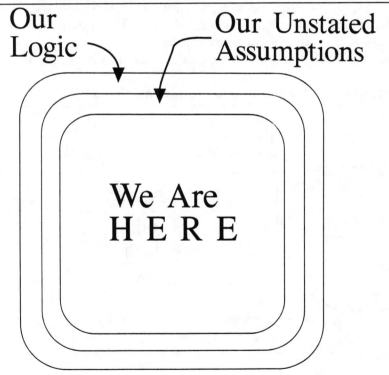

break out of the box of logic and assumptions that controls our thoughts. We call these *trigger tools*—that is, tools that trigger unexpected ideas.

Refer now to Figure 4–2, which shows that we begin any thinking journey inside our thinking box. Before we can break out of this box, we must empty it of all ideas. This is done by "brainstorming to exhaustion," a process we covered in the last chapter. We then use a *trigger tool* to break our thinking patterns, so we can exit the box and generate new and unexpected thoughts.

Of course, many times these unexpected ideas will simply not be useful. They may seem too outrageous, too ridiculous, or too illegal to be considered. The temptation will be to dismiss them outright; however, if we suspend our convergent judgment for a few seconds, and ask, "What is right about this thought?" we may be able to mold the idea into something that's both unexpected *and* useful—something that will help us achieve bottom-line business results.

Although the current literature on creativity lists a great

Figure 4–2. Mechanism to break thinking patterns.

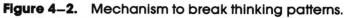

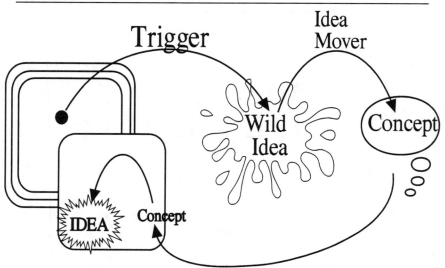

many techniques that can be used to stimulate ideas, we have found that most can be classified into one of a few pattern-breaking, "trigger" categories.

FOUR BASIC "TRIGGERS" YOU CAN USE

1. Forcing Associations

This technique forces us to make an association between two unlike things. As a result of the association, we generate new ideas that we would otherwise not have had. The first step in this process is to locate a concept that we can use to help force the association. This concept can be drawn from a word selected at random from a book, newspaper, or dictionary; from a photograph in a magazine; or from objects found in a room, a museum, a shopping mall, etc. (For this reason, it's sometimes helpful to take an excursion to a museum, go for a walk in the woods, or head to a mall during a "creativity" session.)

How, exactly, does forcing associations work? Consider the example of one company that wanted to eliminate the accidental release of hydrogen fluoride gas from process piping. The problem-solving participants picked several words at random from the dictionary, one of which was "earwax." They agreed that earwax was a self-protecting mechanism the body used to keep bacteria from the ears. This led them to ponder how they could make their pumps and lines "self-protecting." Suddenly one chemist shouted, "Calcium gluconate!" He explained that people neutralize HF contamination on their hands by washing with this solution. Ultimately, he proposed the unexpected and highly promising idea of using calcium gluconate at the joints of pipes to neutralize any accidental release of gas.

2. Reversing Hidden Assumptions

This technique brings to the forefront the hidden assumptions about our problem or situation that we have never bothered to examine, then centers in on several of those assumptions and examines what would happen if circumstances were reversed. For example, suppose that you own a computer store, and you hear that a huge computer discount chain is coming to your area. Your challenge is to preserve, or perhaps even grow, your business in the face of stiff price competition. Using the reversing hidden assumptions technique, you would list all of your basic assumptions about computer stores, about your business, and about your customers. Your list might begin with such hidden assumptions as:

1. My store sells new computers.
2. My store sells software.
3. Customers pay for the computers they purchase.

Next, you would start reversing those assumptions that seem provocative, then explore the reversed statements to see what ideas might emerge. For example, you might decide to reverse the third assumption on the list, coming up with the statement, "Customers *don't* pay for their computers." Playing with this idea, you might ask yourself, "Who would pay instead?" The answer could be local companies or local computer clubs. Concentrating on the first option, you might think about striking a deal: You give local companies quantity discounts on computers, and suggest that they offer their employees low- or no-interest loans to purchase the computers at the lower price. In this way, you would have used the reversing-assumptions technique to expand your market despite new pricing pressures!

3. Metaphorical Thinking

This technique seeks to compare our problem or situation with that of a natural or well-known system, so we can identify gaps in our situation and fill them with unexpected ideas. For example, consider one raw-materials supplier that had a *very* difficult customer, who tended to dictate prices, quality levels, and delivery schedules. Essentially, this customer was running a portion of the supplier's business! And because the customer purchased some 40 percent of the supplier's production—and had threatened in the past to begin making its own raw materials—the customer's demands just couldn't be ignored. The supplier's problem statement was, "How might we make this customer an ally instead of an enemy?"

Using metaphoric thinking, the supplier selected the natural system of a garden with which to make comparisons. The problem-solving participants listed the components of a garden down the left side of a flip-chart pad, then listed the corresponding elements of their business to the right:

THE GARDEN	THE PROBLEM
Plants	Our facilities
Water, fertilizer	Raw materials
Soil	Working capital
Fruits	Our products
A Gardener	Business director
Sun	Customer demand
Insects	Regulations
Weeds	Competitors
A Scarecrow	?
Harvest	Profits

Participants could come up with no counterpart to the garden's scarecrow; so they asked themselves, "How might we generate a 'scarecrow' in our business to help us turn this difficult customer into an ally?" They realized that they were familiar with a way for their company to "forward integrate"—that is, to take its own output and convert it into products similar to those sold by the customer. Thus, their "scarecrow" could be a patent on the process that would allow the company to forward integrate, thereby competing with this difficult customer. The firm filed the patent and showed it to the customer, who reportedly became concerned and grew far more compliant as a result.

A number of other metaphors can also work well for companies who want to try this technique, such as a beehive, a circus, a train, the medical system, and so on.

4. The Outrageous Idea

This technique uses outrageous suggestions—ideas you would never implement because they are illegal, immoral, wicked, or downright disgusting—to "relocate" us to a position outside our thinking box. Using this technique, we must be careful to suspend judgment, since the outrageous ideas generated are truly "out of the box." As an example, consider a consulting company in downtown New York City, which called together its worldwide marketing managers so they could learn about pattern-breaking thinking and generate ideas on how to attract new customers for their seminars. After some prodding, one manager came up with an outrageous suggestion: "I've got it!" she said. "Let's provide every customer with a free sleep-over date for the evening!"

After the participants had calmed down (truly outrageous ideas will usually lead people to laugh, gasp, or wince), they agreed that the actual concept expressed by that outrageous idea was, "Let's give our customers more than they bargained for." The group played with that idea for a while, until another manager said, "I know—let's have a staff person stand in line at the half-price ticket booth in Times Square, and we'll offer every new customer a half-price ticket to a Broadway show!" In all its years of existence, this organization had never before conceived of this kind of unexpected and useful idea.

WHEN TO USE WHICH?

You may be wondering when you should use each tool. Unfortunately, there is no easy answer. In practice, some of the tools will work better than others. The variables seem to be (1) the nature of the problem statement, (2) the style of the meeting facilitator, (3) the styles of participants, and (4) the energy level of participants. A good strategy is to begin with reversing hidden assumptions, move to forcing associations, then to the outrageous idea, and finally to metaphoric thinking. In most idea-generating sessions, however, there will likely be time for only two or three of the tools.

Keep in mind that using *any* of these tools requires considerable energy, so meetings should take place when participants are rested and fresh. Otherwise it's like driving up a steep mountain when the gas tank is all but empty: Don't start—you won't make it to the top, and you may have to back down.

5

The Working Environment

Just as our natural environment may be healthy or unhealthy, so too may the organizational environment in which we work. If an atmosphere of mistrust, fear of failure, and enforced conformity prevails, employees will not be innovative—not even if the organization provides "innovation training" or leaders exhort employees to "be innovative." Many leaders believe that inspiring employees to be innovative is the responsibility of the training staff; in reality, however, it is the environment (or the climate)—*which the leaders themselves create*—that is perhaps the single biggest factor governing the success of the organization's total innovation effort.

As an example of how an organization's climate can encourage innovation, refer to the box on page 41. You'll see that the USDA Forest Service, Eastern Region, documented an 18 percent improvement in productivity by developing a climate in which employees were encouraged to develop and implement ideas. Clearly, the effort paid off, and Vice President Al Gore's recent report, "Creating A Government That Works Better & Costs Less," recognizes the region's efforts to build a creative, people-oriented work climate as one of the positive examples of reinventing Government.

Changing the Working Environment: The Case of the USDA Forest Service, Eastern Region

For the USDA Forest Service, Eastern Region, headquartered in Milwaukee, an effort to change the rigid, inflexible organizational culture has yielded an 18 percent boost in productivity, as well as greatly improved customer service.

The effort, started in the late 1980s, spearheaded by Floyd "Butch" Marita, regional forester and leader of the 15 national forests in the east.

Marita recounts that in initiating the effort, his primary goal was to "draw upon the brain power of everyone." He reasoned that "people who thrive on ambiguity, freedom, and a loose operating style, along with making things happen, are going to have an exciting time." *Project Spirit* was the name given to Marita's program, which solicited employee ideas, allowed them to test the ideas, and take risks to implement them. *Project Spirit* has paid off. In one four-year period, employees came up with more than 12,000 ideas—which helped streamline work, increase the region's effectiveness and efficiency, cut red tape, improve customer service, and save taxpayers' money. For example, one idea by a Contract Specialist, Bill Millard, to streamline purchase-order processing generated a savings of more than $500,000. His idea was to create a simple check-writing process called "third-party drafts" that eliminated the need for the complex Federal purchasing process for small purchases under $2500. Overall, the region has saved nearly $3 million annually as a result of employee ideas, Marita says.

Marita's interest in employee input has produced a new, entrepreneurial spirit in the region—very rare for a government organization. He proudly asserts that the organization today values shared leadership, empowerment, teamwork, and quality.

For more information on this effort, contact Karl Mettke, USDA Forest Service, Eastern Region, Room 500, 310 West Wisconsin Ave., Milwaukee, WI 53203

THE NINE DIMENSIONS OF THE WORKING ENVIRONMENT

Of the various research that has been conducted on how a work environment supports creativity and innovation, the most intriguing—and potentially most useful—is that pioneered by Göran Ekvall[1] in Sweden. Ekvall's original research, which identified ten dimensions of the organizational climate, led to the development of the Climate for Innovation Questionnaire (CIQ), an instrument for measuring climate. The questionnaire was validated in Sweden using eight companies termed "innovative" in products and services vs four termed "stagnant" and now out of business. Scott Isaksen[2], director, Center for Studies in Creativity, SUNY, Buffalo, NY, brought the CIQ to the United States and refined its use, with a specific focus on nine dimensions.

The nine dimensions are summarized below (for a more complete overview, see the Appendix):

- *Challenge and Involvement.* (How challenged, how emotionally involved, and how committed am I to the work?)
- *Freedom.* (How free am I to decide how to do my job?)
- *Idea Time.* (Do we have time to think things through before having to act?)
- *Idea Support.* (Do we have resources to give a new idea a try?)
- *Conflict.* (To what degree do people engage in interpersonal conflict, sometimes characterized as "warfare?") Note: This is the only dimension that is negatively correlated with a climate supporting innovation.
- *Debates.* (Do people engage in lively debates or discussions about the issues, sharing different points of view?)
- *Humor and Playfulness.* (Is our workplace relaxed, a place where it's okay to have fun?)
- *Trust and Openness.* (Do people feel safe in speaking their minds and openly putting forward different points of view?)
- *Risk Taking.* (Is it okay to fail trying out new things?)

Evidence is mounting on the CIQ's potential usefulness. Validation studies for North America, under the direction of Scott Isaksen, provide strong anecdotal defense for the idea that a supportive climate correlates with innovation, productivity, and job satisfaction. Consider one such anecdote.

Gerard Puccio, in collaboration with Isaksen, studied a prominent U.S. automobile manufacturer using the CIQ. He found that two back-to-back shifts, which were responsible for identical work of forging automobile parts, showed widely different climates. The climate of the first shift, managed by a supervisor who was not open to new ideas, was deficient in most of the nine variables. Before the CIQ study began, one of the workers on this shift caught a problem with the metal that was being processed for a part and reported it to the supervisor. The supervisor's response was incisive: "You're not paid to find problems." He ignored the problem and the machine ran that entire shift. When the shift was over, the workers discovered they had to scrap every part made that day because of the problem the worker had identified.

In sharp contrast, the climate measurements of the second shift showed strengths in most of the nine dimensions. Their supervisor took a supportive, enabling approach and was open to new ideas. These workers self-describe themselves as "creatively productive," and they routinely handled issues such as the quality problem described above.

The difference between the two groups showed most clearly when news came that the plant had been sold. The second shift took the attitude of "whatever happens, we will continue doing our jobs well." Workers on the first shift were distraught; the news virtually destroyed their willingness to carry on with their jobs.

(Note: To obtain additional information on Puccio's research, as well as on the various company programs described in this chapter, see "For More Information" at the end of the chapter.)

TOOLS FOR INFLUENCING CLIMATE

If you believe your climate for innovation needs attention, you might well ask, "How should we get started?"

An excellent example of how leadership can improve climate comes from a West Coast consumer products company. The vice president of R&D felt a need to improve the climate for innovation as a prelude to greater emphasis on new product development. As in any organization, improvement was needed, and the results of the CIQ assessment pinpointed several areas.

To follow up, the vice president organized focused problem-solving meetings to decide what specific actions would be taken in the areas identified. Seventy-three employees from throughout the organization "brainstormed to exhaustion," ultimately generating 1,483 specific ideas!

At that point, the employees engaged in pattern-breaking thinking, generating an additional 1,032 ideas. Although this effort has just begun, people are enthusiastically contributing their ideas and have volunteered for climate improvement teams. Each team has responsibility for one major climate dimension, and they are busy refining and implementing specific ideas. The organization plans to re-test the climate in one to two years, to measure progress and to identify the next most important areas of the climate to address.

The Marketing arm of the same company learned of the broad innovation initiative of the R&D arm and used the *Bottom Line Innovation* process described in Chapter 3 to develop new ideas for product line renewal. Some 50 people representing cross-functional groups produced 1,951 ideas in seven market areas. This sent a clear message, that taking time up-front to think of new and unexpected ideas was valued. Recall, Idea Time is one of the nine dimensions of the Climate for Innovation.

For organizations that are eager to make their own climate more innovative, we offer one piece of essential advice: Begin to evaluate your climate *only if you intend to follow through by implementing specific improvement ideas.* The act of measuring an organizational climate changes it. After all, people tend to expect the climate to improve if management has gone to the trouble of measuring it, and when things do not improve, the climate will actually become worse.

Consider the case of one Midwest R&D firm, which measured its climate for creativity and innovation but did not act on the findings. Employees felt "used" because their input was sought but nothing was done, and a few reported increased cynicism at management's commitment to improve.

Although using an instrument like the CIQ can pinpoint clear areas for improvement, many firms have improved the climate without first assessing it. Below we give several outstanding examples; each provides concepts that you may wish to use as part of your blueprint for innovation.

Consider what Sam Safrit, former vice president of R&D for Kayser Roth, a major hosiery manufacturer, did to set an environment for creativity and innovation. He put out the call to everyone in his organization for ideas on how to improve anything related to the business—no areas were "off limits" for improvement. He tabulated the ideas, and once a month invited those who had contributed the most ideas that month (typically 30–40 people) to a one-hour catered lunch.

During lunch, Safrit would teach one creativity technique, then present a problem facing the business and ask participants to use the new technique to generate ideas to solve the problem. One session, involving some 40 participants, generated over 1,000 ideas within the allotted 60 minutes! His initiative built employee enthusiasm and involvement and produced bottom line results. A small sampling of the results include ideas for new products, new marketing and sales approaches, and new ways to improve existing work. Sam exclaims that the business results from the ideas that were implemented were overwhelming!

Another unique example comes from 3M, a company long known for innovation. Several of 3M's divisions now use an "Ideas Database" to capture and put ideas to work. The 3M

Home Products Division, for example, set up and began capturing ideas in the Ideas Database in 1982. As John Rueb, technical director of the 3M Consumer Stationery Division, describes it:

> We were getting ideas from people all the time. The problem was, they were only as useful as they were retained. We decided to capture all ideas in a computerized database so we could draw upon them in the future, either as they were initially offered, or as a springboard for something else. The Ideas Database now has accumulated more than 11,000 ideas!

Several divisions of 3M now follow the practice of capturing all ideas from whatever source, in whatever form they are contributed. The Ideas Database can be searched by key word, by subject matter, by technology, and by "type of application," such as technology, packaging, or process. When ideas are needed on a particular subject, an employee can search the Ideas Database and use the output either directly, or to spark additional ideas in a brainstorming session.

Use of the database also allows 3M to connect with the original suggester, since his or her name is attached to the idea. When someone submits an idea for the database, the system produces a one-page printout that describes the idea. This is sent to the suggester as proof that 3M was listening. Any employee can give a hand-written idea to the system administrator, who will enter it into the Ideas Database. Alternatively, any employee with computer access may enter ideas or perform searches themselves.

John Rueb recognizes three levels of idea maturity. The first level is the raw material, the simple idea statement that may have been produced in a idea session. The second maturity level is a refined idea with a headline and a two- or three-sentence description as it would normally be entered into the Ideas Database. The third level occurs when there is a fully formed new product concept. These are summarized on a one-page *New Product Proposal* with a title and a headline describing the essence of the idea. The next four sections of the proposal describe (1) the problem being addressed, (2) the product form envisioned, (3) how the product might be used by the customer, and (4) what the benefit to the customer might be. *New Product Proposals* are put into a book form and are also entered into the Ideas Database.

3M has traced the results of using the system, and John Rueb can point to a large number of profitable products that had their origins in the database. In some cases, ideas that were not right at the time they were proposed were retrieved several years later, resulting in innovative products that were business successes.

RISK TAKING: THE GREAT WALL BARRING INNOVATION

Of the nine dimensions listed above, risk taking is probably the most important. When an employee's career is damaged, or he or she is publicly embarrassed as a result of an implementation that didn't meet expectations, the rest of the organization gets the message: *Don't fail.* As a result, people will be reluctant to take all but the smallest steps in implementing ideas, and will go only for the sure "hits," leaving the quantum-leap developments to the competition.

How can an organization's leaders know if they are unwittingly sending the "Don't Fail" message? For one thing, they should consider whether they speak of having a "tolerance for risk" and/or advise employees to take "prudent risks." Both of these messages really mean, "Don't Fail."

Leaders should also consider how they respond to "nice tries" that don't meet expectations. Do they search for the guilty and fix blame, or do they search for the facts and "fix learning?" The instant that blame is fixed, future risk taking is inhibited.

How can an organization's leaders send consistent messages of support for risk taking—and, consequently, for the innovation process? They should start first by understanding that in developing and implementing anything new, employees will make mistakes. For this reason, the company must adopt a philosophy of *expecting mistakes*. Managers must respect the learning that results when mistakes happen, and must reward individuals and teams that have had the fortitude to try new ideas—especially when the ideas don't meet expectations. It's also a good idea for organizations to reword their vision or mission statement, adding a phrase such as, "We expect people to take risks to improve the company's health," or "We expect mistakes and will value them for the lessons they teach, rather than blaming individuals."

Of course, these new additions must be lived daily as work is done; they can not become meaningless words on paper. Leaders lead by example, so one thing leaders might do is to admit their own mistakes first and engage their groups in learning from them.

Finally, managers should consider how their own performance might be different if their boss were to say, "I expect you to take risks that make sense to you. If things don't go as expected, I'll take the heat." Nearly all the people we've spoken to have said they would take greater risks, and would go to extremes to help assure that every risk taken had a favorable outcome, since they would not want to lose such an enabling leader.

THE ELEMENTS OF CULTURE

Culture—that is, the implicit, fundamental assumptions that employees hold about appropriate patterns of thinking and behaving—is often described as the glue that holds an organization together. An organization's culture includes many components. Among these are:

• *Values*—the activities or business outcomes that a company feels are of utmost importance. An organization's values may include going to extraordinary lengths to satisfy a customer, finding continuous ways to drive down expenses, or providing a quality product or service for a unique market niche.

• *Norms*—the should's, ought's, and must's of organizational life. Cultural norms are reflected in the messages an organization sends out regarding how employees should work together and interact with one another.

• *Symbolic Representations*—the observable features of an organization's culture that indicate what the organization stands for. Such symbols may include the physical layout of the facility, decorations, photographs, etc.

• *Other Indicators of Culture*—the written and/or verbal expressions and ongoing events that provide formative learning experiences to company members. Such indicators can include corporate belief statements, stories repeated by employees and customers, and rituals such as award ceremonies, company celebrations, and social gatherings.

Of course, within any organization, different departments may have different values or norms that apply to that particular group. The accounting department, for example, may emphasize precision, measurement, and control to a greater extent than other departments do. However, it's critical that organizational leaders point everyone in the same direction and make sure everyone knows his or her role in the overall drama. They must help all employees realize that the organization's collective values and norms contribute far more to the company's effectiveness than those of any single unit. We call this task *creating cultural synergy*.

To understand how the elements of an organization's culture work together, refer to the model of culture shown in Figure 5–1. At the center of the model is top management's *vision* for the company. The vision includes the organization's purpose and mission: whom it serves in a marketplace, the products or services with which it serves, and the way that it

Figure 5–1. Culture model: From vision to symbol.

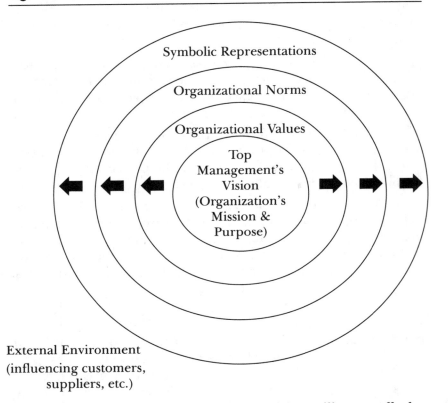

Symbolic Representations

Organizational Norms

Organizational Values

Top
Management's
Vision
(Organization's
Mission &
Purpose)

External Environment
(influencing customers,
suppliers, etc.)

delivers these goods or services. This vision will generally be reflected in the next circle in the model: the company's values. Finally, if the organization has successfully communicated its vision and values, they will affect the other circles: organizational norms and symbolic representations.

The model in Figure 5–1 is particularly helpful for organizations that want to create a culture that reinforces creative thinking and behavior. For this kind of effort, the first step is to assess the elements of the existing culture, then analyze the messages they are actually sending. To do this, the organization's leaders should refer to the model and determine which elements of their organization's culture are currently sending an identifiable, distinct, and clear message about creativity and innovation to employees.

THE ROLE OF CULTURAL NORMS

Norms—the expected ways for employees to act and interact—are where culture comes to life in an organization. They are the primary way in which culture is internalized and passed throughout the company. What are the norms that employees may observe at work? Here are some examples.

In one large electrical manufacturing company, a newly hired engineer was attending his first divisional meeting. About ten minutes into the meeting, a latecomer entered the room and quietly slipped into the first available chair so as not to disturb the others. At this, the director in charge of the meeting stopped speaking, looked at the latecomer, and said curtly, "You can't sit there. That's the vice president's chair."

Even though the VP was not there, the latecomer rose and edged his way past several people to reach another unoccupied chair. The director's actions revealed something important about this organization's culture: The chairs in this company were not created equal—and neither, by extension, were the employees.

It's doubtful whether ideas submitted by lower-level employees would have even been considered, let alone valued, in this firm.

Another scenario: At one medical products manufacturer, which had posters that read "THINK!" on the plant walls, a technician approached his foreman with an idea for increasing efficiency. The foreman listened, shrugged his shoulders, and said he'd bring it up at a plant meeting. The technician waited patiently for two months, then decided to stop in to see the plant manager. The plant manager listened to his idea, looked him squarely in the eye, and said, "You're not paid to think." Clearly, in this firm, management was simply not interested in generating creativity among employees, despite the signs it had posted.

Now for another side to the picture—this experience was recounted by another new hire, this time with a telecommunications company. "I was putting some circuitry together with my supervisor, and I was told, 'In order to make an omelette, you have to break a few eggs.' My supervisor's support of me made me feel that I could make mistakes and learn from them." In this organization, the recruit felt valued—a feeling that would likely lead to creativity and innovation. It's important, however, that managers in firms like this *consistently* support learning and experimentation. If they betray their employees' trust, even during seemingly trivial or informal conversations, they will do serious damage to the culture.

Now that you've considered the cultural norms operating in other organizations, take a closer look at what goes on in your own firm. For example:

1. How do managers communicate with their employees? By memo, by e-mail, in person, or in small-group meetings? The more direct and personal the interactions, the more effectively thoughts can be articulated and understanding can be confirmed.

2. Do employees feel comfortable (1) asking questions of their managers, or even of customers? (2) making mistakes and trying over? (3) admitting they are wrong? (4) asking for advice? Norms that support learning, questioning, experimenting, and trying are building blocks for a culture of innovation.

3. If an employee finds a "better" (i.e., faster, snazzier, bigger, smaller, more colorful, more durable) way of doing something, can he or she "change the system"? It's hard to believe the inertia that exists in some companies—or worse, the deliberate obstacles management puts in place to slow down any change, no matter how small. We recall a marketing director who told us that by the time all the required management signatures had been obtained to approve a new idea, the idea had generally become obsolete.

Many organizations have erected very high organizational

barriers to innovation, usually in the form of bureaucracy. These barriers effectively slow the process, sometimes to a halt. This helps assure greater success to those competitors with fewer barriers. Removing—or at least significantly lowering—organizational barriers to innovation will be a crucial element of your blueprint for innovation.

Consider DuPont's approach to overcoming organizational barriers to innovation. Their "$EED Program" was established 10 years ago in response to an internal innovation audit that revealed implementation as the major barrier to innovation at DuPont. The $EED program grants money to full-time DuPont employees who have good ideas and a strong desire to "make it happen," but whose business unit has not been able to fund. In the 10-year history of the program, DuPont has expended some $2.9 million to $EED ideas, and has realized over $20 million in additional revenue from the product or service ideas that were implemented.

The financial success of the program should not obscure the highest value DuPont places on the program; setting an environment that promotes giving ideas a try by removing organizational barriers. Any DuPont employee can submit a request for a $EED grant.

The single-page application (reproduced in Figure 5-2 through the courtesy of DuPont) is reviewed by the $EED Committee—a group of volunteer senior professionals who decide on funding. Since the program's beginning in 1986, some 700 requests for $EED grants have been processed, with some 40 percent being funded at an average final grant of about $10,000 each. Awardees decide on expenditures, which usually include travel, experimental equipment, and supplies, but do not include pay. The awardee must account for funds expended at the end of the project; he or she can request an additional grant if needed, or can return any unused funds.

Ira Hill, former vice president for technology at International Fragrances and Flavors, provides another example. His experience illustrates that focusing on innovative ideas for new products can, in itself, overcome organizational barriers.

Figure 5–2. The DuPont $eed grant.

$EED GRANT APPLICATION

Dollars to Encourage Entrepreneurial Developments

Return to: $EED, Experimental Station, Bldg. 326/Room 315

Name: _____   Department: _____

Job Title: _____   Address: _____   Telephone: _____

Current program assignment/SBU: _____

Title of idea: _____   Amount requested: _____

Explanation of market need and your idea: _____

_____

_____

_____

How does your idea fit with DuPont's strengths and interests? _____

_____

_____

Milestones to be accomplished with this grant, including timing and resources needed to accomplish them
(include, if possible, a summary of how you would allocate $EED funds):

_____

_____

_____

Have you considered patent protection for your idea? _____

_____

_____

What other resources (funding or in-kind contributions) would be
available to you from your SBU or elsewhere in DuPont?

_____

_____

_____

Signature: _____

Date: _____

(Please attach additional Information or sketches, If necessary, to support your business plan)

DUPONT

For $EED Comittee Use Only

Grant # _____   Amount _____

Contact _____   Date _____

Ira reports that soon after he joined IFF in the mid-1970s, economic conditions worsened. He faced the task of large scale lay-offs, an air conditioning system that failed during the hottest summer on record, and understandably, low employee morale. During the three weeks the air conditioning system was being repaired, Ira decided to hold brainstorming meetings every morning to which every interested person, regardless of level, was invited. The trigger question was "I think IFF should develop _____." He tape-recorded the sessions and had every idea transcribed. The ten most frequently mentioned ideas were collated and sent to every employee in R&D.

Due to pressures on the job, Ira forgot about the list until six years later, when one of the R&D directors found the list while cleaning out his desk to move to a new office. Both executives were surprised to find that of the ten ideas, six had become profitable commercial products! In Ira's words, the lesson is clear, "When people make creative suggestions and know that other creative people have been listening and are thinking along the same lines, informal cooperation triggers the kind of practical demonstrations which grow into fully justified projects." Think how you might use this principle in your firm.

Improving the climate for innovation can be especially effective if initiated and supported from the top of the organization. Consider, for example, how Skip Ulmer, vice president and general manager of business development at Schuller International, Inc., confronted potentially disastrous business conditions. Skip recalls:

In 1991 Schuller International, Inc. evolved from the 100-plus-year-old shadow of Johns Manville Corporation, which had just completed restructuring as a result of a 1982 bankruptcy filing based on asbestos litigation. Schuller's fiberglass-based products in insulation, filtration, and building materials were very depressed, losing some $20 million during its first year of operation on sales of $1 billion. Schuller could no longer just wait on the market to recover.

The first step was a reduction of $100 million in costs—cutting the workforce by 25 percent and moth-balling high-cost production.

Like other executives recruited from corporations like GE and DuPont, Skip helped establish a new culture by focusing on the company's core production and market strengths. As financial results improved, he recognized that new products and new market strategies would be essential for long-term growth and profitability.

Borrowing from the 50-year-old success story of Kelly Johnson and the SkunkWorks philosophy at Lockheed, Skip introduced a "SkunkWorks" program at Schuller. A key element of this successful program is the monthly *SkunkWorks Newsletter*, each issue publicizing and celebrating one or two stories of Schuller innovations that have achieved commercial status. Objectives of the newsletter are simple: (1) to increase the awareness of innovation via corporate recognition of the "SkunkWorks" teams, and (2) to stimulate and encourage new ideas for innovative products.

The company went on to create a "SkunkWorks" logo, develop a tag line (*"SKUNKWORKS, A Schuller State Mind"*), and establish a "SkunkWorks Wall-of-Fame" in the lobby of corporate headquarters. Each individual so honored receives a remembrance of his or her accomplishment and membership in the "SkunkWorks Community."

What about results? Skip says that Schuller is currently seeing more than $10 million annually in new sales traceable to SkunkWorks innovations. One such innovation is Insul-Mide Polyimide Foam. Its unique blend of acoustic and thermal insulation, light weight, and low smoke, non-burn characteristics make it ideally suited for insulating ship bulkheads, ceilings, and hulls. Sales continue to grow significantly each year.

A benefit as important as any other is expressed well by Bill Plichta, business manager, who notes, "Starting a new business from laboratory bench top to full commercialization has been the most challenging—but at the same time, the rewarding—

experience of my career. The success to date is attributed to the commitment and talent of the team and being able to operate as an entrepreneur in a corporate environment."

Skip emphasizes that Innovation is a journey, not a destination. He expects financial benefits from the SkunkWorks effort to grow to $50 million in five years. More importantly, however, he notes that individual motivation for innovation has improved, and says that financial growth will be a direct reflection of the climate for innovation. In 1994, Schuller recorded $159 million in earnings . . . quite a change from the losses of 1991. And the SkunkWorks philosophy is in place for future growth, product innovation and corporate success.

And leaders also need to keep in mind that "freedom to change the system" refers not just to how work is performed, but to where it is performed as well. Many people prefer not to be confined to a carrel or office all day to complete their work. We know of several companies that encourage telecommuting and staying in touch electronically. Is it just a coincidence that these are some of the most innovative and responsive companies around?

By contrast, how many managers do you know who believe they must constantly monitor their employees to make sure they are working? Such a philosophy sends the message to employees that their manager doesn't trust them—that he or she believes they will surely be unproductive, even irresponsible, if they are out of sight or away from the office.

Instead, managers should realize that the freedom to be away from the office might lead employees to develop numerous ideas they otherwise would never have developed. Being away from the office might mean visiting a customer or two, even a competitor or two at a trade show or professional meeting. Getting out and talking with others (even those who work down the hall, with another team or in another department) can refresh and stimulate people. By loosening the reins on employees, companies will be instituting a norm that supports an innovative culture.

THE ROLE OF SYMBOLIC REPRESENTATIONS

Look around your department and the rest of the organization. What colors, textures, sounds, and visual images do you observe? Symbolic representations, though the most superficial of all the elements of culture, can play an important role in reinforcing deeper values and norms. And if they contradict important values and norms, they can work against the company's goals.

A case in point: In an effort to set clear expectations regarding quality and effective problem solving, one chemical company sponsored training programs in these areas. Yet several employees who attended such sessions said it was nearly impossible to be motivated to use their newly honed skills. Even though their leaders were supportive, they said, they were surrounded everyday by brown, worn carpeting, brown paint on the walls, no pictures, no plants, etc. Sound inspiring? Not in the least!

Inexpensive touches, such as a coat of paint, framed posters, and a few plants, can go a long way toward creating a working environment that nurtures creativity and innovation. Conference rooms with round tables, which have no obvious head, and at which everyone can see and hear one another clearly, are also helpful. Studies show that such low-cost improvements can actually yield great returns.

BUILDING THE CREATIVE CULTURE

We have seen that to build a company culture that embraces creative thinking and behavior, an organization must institute a set of norms that reinforces curiosity, experimentation, and learning. A *prohibitive* culture—that is, one that keeps things from happening—can be compared with an *inquisitive* culture—that is, one that seeks to discover what's right about new ideas and concepts—in the following way:

Prohibitive Culture	Inquisitive Culture
Encourages formal meetings and interactions.	Encourages informal meetings and interactions.
Expects and rewards only success.	Recognizes and rewards "nice tries."
Encourages employees to hold knowledge closely.	Encourages employees to share knowledge freely.
Frowns on risk taking.	Values risk taking.
Reinforces behaviors that uphold tradition.	Reinforces behaviors that question tradition.
Encourages managers to closely monitor work time.	Encourages managers to be flexible about work time.
Focuses on short-term performance.	Focuses on long-term performance.
Encourages employees to interact with insiders only.	Encourages employees to interact with customers and people in other departments.

For an organization to become more creative and innovative, it must have an inquisitive culture. How does an organization move from the prohibitive to the inquisitive? A good place to start is by reviewing the mistakes companies make when trying to be creative, which we covered in Chapter 2, and turning them into positives. For example, when a group of individuals approach any problem-solving situation, the prevailing culture should encourage them to:

• *Be sure they've defined the right problem.* When this is a true cultural norm, people will never stop with the first definition; instead, they will continue to ask, "What else might the problem be?" and "What might be the root cause?" Somebody may even ask, "Wouldn't it be nice if . . ."

- **Defer judgment of ideas.** As we discussed earlier, educated people tend to jump to conclusions—usually negative ones—about why something won't work. The ideal norm would be for people automatically to ask, "What is right?"—that is, for people to defer judgment and explore all options before making any decisions.

- **Insist on more than one good idea.** Employees should come up with a number of options to a problem, then discuss why one should be selected over the others.

- **Find sponsors for their ideas.** An organization's cultural norms should provide strong support for employees to seek "champions" at higher levels within the organization. By doing this, they make sure the "bandits are on their train" before they start their journey, which would greatly increase their chances of success.

After identifying the most desirable values and norms, companies then must institutionalize those cultural components. For example, consider how DuPont is focusing on making things happen. Robin Karol, Manager, Renewal Processes, says that DuPont is focusing on the growth and renewal of its businesses through the use of structured processes.

DuPont found that to maintain an environment that encourages continued innovation and contribution of new ideas, there must be a visible process to move these concepts quickly and enable the commercialization of new products. DuPont has established a best practice for the development and commercialization of new products and processes; PACE (Product and Cycle Time Excellence).

This business process, originally obtained from Pittiglio, Rabin, Todd, and McGrath, a consulting company in Weston, MA, and described in McGrath, et al.[3], utilizes cross-functional development teams and a cross-functional decision-making group. DuPont has evolved the PACE process to handle a broader range of growth and renewal initiatives. Using this process, DuPont has improved cycle time some 40–60 percent while improving quality and optimizing business success.

The PACE process also improves communication between the functions as well as between the business leaders, functional leaders, and the development teams through the phase review process. Employee morale and enthusiasm has improved and individuals now feel more involved in the business process, making them more likely to participate in the renewal of the business. This connection with the business process is one of the nine dimensions (Challenge and Involvement) of the Climate for Innovation.

Another example of institutionalizing the most desirable values and norms is shown by R. R. Donnelley Companies, which is presented in the box on page 62.

WHAT ABOUT SUGGESTION SYSTEMS?

In an employee satisfaction audit conducted more than a decade ago at a major East Coast chemical company, an hourly employee at a plant location responded, "For 20 years you have paid for my hands, and you could have had my head for free, but you never asked." What a call to action for organizations around the world!

As a means of enabling employees to use their brains, and not just their hands, many companies use suggestion systems. However, these often fall short of capturing the most compelling employee ideas and input. Why? Often the problem is that companies don't use the most effective approach for them. Managers often don't know which routes to take when they start to ask themselves such questions as "Should we pay for suggestions?" "How should we solicit ideas from employees?" "Who should judge and select ideas?" and "How quickly should we give feedback to the suggester?"

For example, Detroit Edison, like most companies, had an ineffective employee suggestion system (their "Employe Proposal Plan"). During its last year in place it garnered less than 200 suggestions from their 9,500 employees (less than 2 percent participation). Unhappy with this level of performance,

Institutionalizing Values and Norms: The Case of R. R. Donnelley & Sons Company

A series of programs developed by R. R. Donnelley & Sons Company provides a useful model on how to use training to accomplish cultural change. R. R. Donnelley is the world's largest commercial printer and a leader in managing, reproducing, and distributing print and digital information for publishing, retailing, merchandising and information technology markets in the United States and around the world. The company employs about 41,000 people in 20 countries on five continents. Stretching a consistent—and effective—corporate culture across time zones and national boundaries is a significant challenge.

To meet this challenge, the company formed the Performance Development Center, a culture-change group charged with developing leadership ability that translates into measurable results: Enhanced corporate financial performance and improved professional and personal growth for the individual. As it states in its formal capabilities brochure, the Center develops "... a new breed of leader who can respond to the company's ambitious growth objectives . . . leaders who will create a vibrant new corporate culture that generates financial success, who will develop an environment of sustained and continuous improvement . . . who are capable of steering the company with vision, integrity, purpose, and the trust of their respective organizations." Lofty goals indeed.

To bring those goals to realization, the Performance Development Center, for example, offers the "Organization Development (OD) Practitioner Certification Process," a program that develops internal consultants from all business sectors who then act as catalysts for cultural transformation and business improvement within their business units. This six-week program, which addresses such issues as improving return on net assets, reducing the cost of quality, enhancing customer satisfaction and improving employee commitment was developed in conjunction with DePaul University Graduate School of Business and Columbia University Graduate School of Business. OD Practitioner applicants are asked to identify improvement opportunities within their divisions—information that helps the Center consultant customize the program for each individual. In addition, participants become part of an ongoing internal consulting network, members of which regularly share best practices and other lessons learned.

"Discovery" is a program aimed at sales and account management personnel, that links customer needs with R. R. Donnelley products and services. A primary component of the program is Discovery Boot Camp, a 12-week coaching and feedback course for major account managers. They get to learn from an internal Discovery Team made up of employees from manufacturing, customer service, marketing and other business units. Boot Camp directs the account manager to cast a wider net over a customer by learning more about the customer's business, by identifying other people within the customer organization who could benefit from R. R. Donnelley's expertise and by seeking strategic link-ups between customer needs and R. R. Donnelley products and services.

The graphic symbol selected for the Performance Development Center is an open door, the traditional sign that a corporation is open to new ideas, to better communications, and to listening to employees and customers. This open door, however, signals that employees will be given the opportunity to improve performance and to contribute to corporate results. This open door Invites the employee to come in and reach his or her greatest potential.

This model for culture change works because it is supported at the highest levels of the company. Training and development programs this comprehensive and this sophisticated require not only dollars, but also commitment and belief—the commitment to remove people from their primary jobs to enable them to train for days or even weeks with the belief that the long-term benefit will offset the short-term cost.

---

the company replaced the system in September 1993 with a program labeled simply "Innovations." After only 14 months, some 17 percent of their employees had submitted over 3,000 ideas, with one-third fully implemented at a savings of more than $16 million.

The older system solicited suggestions only in the cost reduction area, whereas the "Innovations" program now asks employees for suggestions in the areas of cost savings, customer satisfaction, quality of work life, and safety. "Innovations" also rewards employees whose ideas get implemented with "points," the number depending on the value of the idea to the company. Points can later be redeemed for merchandise at local stores. While a system like this necessarily creates paperwork, Detroit Edison thinks "Innovations" has paid off handsomely in employee involvement and improvements to the bottom line.

Yet another approach is taken by W.L. Gore & Associates, Inc., a firm widely recognized as highly innovative. Company spokesperson Heidi Cofran says that there is no one "Gore" suggestion system. Rather, individual plants have developed their own. One particular plant with high participation and implementation offers rewards for *participation* rather than awards for the suggestions themselves. As part of its Improvement Opportunity Identification (IOI) program, the plant randomly draws several prize winners from the collected suggestions each month. While all participating associates (Gore's term for its employees) are recognized at plant meetings, the associate with the most improvement submissions in the past year receives special recognition. Most of the suggestions come from production and support associates, but a cooperative effort of associates from different groups, including shop, engineering, and plant leadership, puts the ideas into action.

In 1994, this plant's associates reached their goal of implementing 250 IOI's in one year. They then "raised the bar" by setting their next goal to 350 implemented ideas, which they expect to meet despite a decline in the number of associates in the plant. They experience an 85 percent implementation rate for suggestions received. Suggestions have ranged from eliminating the distraction of squeaky cart wheels and improving ergonomics to ideas for reducing manufacturing downtime and improving maintenance procedures, to highlight a few.

The plant is pleased that suggestions come from a range of associates, not from just one repeat group. The program encourages associates to keep their eyes and ears open and to take nothing for granted. It empowers associates to make change happen, reinforces the concept of continuous improvement, leading to innovative thinking.

The plant is nearing its third year of the program and has seen steady increase in the number of ideas implemented per associate: the first year averaged one implemented suggestion per associate, the second year saw two implemented suggestions per associate, and this year they already have three implemented suggestions per associate. They are aiming ever higher; some Japanese average over 40 suggestions per employee per year, and this plant wants to approach that level.

The Gore culture also encourages associates to make changes on their own, without ever filling out a suggestion form. Gore feels certain this is happening, but often these changes are not tracked and may go without formal recognition. Gore believes they may well be equally or possibly more valuable than the formally suggested ideas.

What kind of suggestion system is right for your company? While most firms will want a system tailored to their specific needs, they should generally design a program that (1) identifies "target" areas of special interest or need for suggestions, (2) is open to all employees, (3) provides rapid feedback, (4) allows everyone in the process from suggestion to implementation to win, (5) celebrates the employee's initiative, creativity, and loyalty, as well as the value of the suggestion to the company, and (6) offers only modest financial rewards (excessive rewards will result in suggestions for only small improvements). All companies will no doubt benefit when they begin asking employees to use their heads as well as their hands!

FOR MORE INFORMATION

The following individuals supplied information for this chapter and have graciously agreed to answer questions about their respective programs:

Dr. Gerard Puccio, Assistant Professor, Center for Studies

in Creativity, Buffalo State University, Chase Hall 244, Buffalo, NY 14222.

Sam Safrit, The Idea Network, 4635 Duffer Ct., Suite A, Pfafftown, NC 27040.

Dr. John Rueb, Technical Director, 3M Consumer Stationery Division, 3M Center, St. Paul, MN 55144-1000.

Dr. Ira Hill, Chairman, Whitehill Oral Technologies, Inc., 950 Highway 36, Hazlet, NJ 07730.

Carol Baker, "Innovations" Coordinator, Detroit Edison, 2000 Second Ave., Detroit, MI 48226.

Dr. Robin A. Karol, Manager Renewal Processes, DuPont, 1007 Market Street, D-11060, Wilmington, DE 19898.

Heidi Cofran, W.L. Gore & Associates, Inc. 551 Paper Mill Road, Newark, DE 19714.

Dr. Skip Ulmer, Vice President and General Manager, Schuller International, Inc., P.O. Box 625005, Littleton, CO 80162-5505.

Mark Plaster, Manager, Performance Capabilities Enhancement, Development Center, R.R. Donnelley & Sons, 1145 Conwell Avenue, Willard, OH 44888.

NOTES

1. Ekvall, G., Arvonen, J., & Waldenstrom-Lindblad, I., *Creative organizational climate; Construction and validation of a measuring instrument* [*Report 2*] (Stockholm: FAradet, 1983). See also, Ekvall, G., "The Climate Metaphor in Organizational Theory," in B. M. Bass and P. J. G. Drenth (Eds.), *Advances in Organizational Psychology: An International Review* (Newbury Park, CA: Sage Publications, 1987). pp. 177–190.
2. Isaksen, S. G., Dorval, K. B., and Treffinger, D. J. *Creative Approaches to Problem Solving* (Dubuque, Iowa: Kendall/Hunt Publishing Company, 1994).
3. Michael E. McGrath, Michael T. Anthony and Amram R. Shapiro, *Product Development: Success Through Product Cycle Time Excellence* (Newton, MA: Butterworth-Heinemann, 1992).

6

Your Personal Problem-Solving Style

About 20 years ago Dr. Michael Kirton, the eminent British psychologist, discovered that an individual's preferred problem-solving—or creativity—style played a great role in determining how that person approached problem-solving.[1] He went on to develop the *Adaptation/Innovation Theory,* which states that a continuum exists between the extremes of high adaption and high innovation, and that an individual's place on the continuum describes how he or she prefers to use creativity to solve problems.

Specifically, he theorized that people at the highly adaptive end of the continuum generally will strive to make an existing system *better*, and are most satisfied when they have jobs that require this type of approach to problem solving. The jobs that fit this preferred style include positions in such fields as dentistry and surgery, where the goal is to fix what is wrong with the existing system, making it better; accounting (versus financial) posts; and most clerical positions. These individuals tend to be viewed as agents of stability—"anchors" for their group or organization.

People at the highly innovative end of the continuum, by contrast, seek to make the existing system *different*, and are most satisfied when they are in jobs that involve new product development, reengineering, or other functions that bring change to the company. The jobs that fit this preferred style are positions where the focus is on research and development; sales and marketing posts; and financial (versus accounting) positions. These individuals tend to be viewed as agents of change and are perceived as more spontaneous and less likely to spend time planning, when compared with their more adaptive partners.

Where an employee falls on the Adaptation/Innovation continuum is a function of who they are. It is not a choice they make. Also, one's creativity style tends to be stable over time. There is no important gender bias and, as far as we know, no cultural bias. There is also no correlation with birth order. Although an individual's style can be reliably measured by the early teens, all indications are that it is set quite early: In fact, differences in style among siblings are apparent by the age of two.

JOB SATISFACTION AND PROBLEM-SOLVING STYLE

What happens if an individual's job responsibilities require a problem-solving style different from the one the person prefers to use? The answer is simple: Although it is impossible to change one's preference, the person must change his or her behavior if the job is to be performed well. Changing one's behavior requires energy: This kind of energy is called *coping energy*. When an employee ends up in a job that requires a less-preferred problem-solving style, it's as if that individual were constantly struggling to carry a heavy load. Clearly, job satisfaction is inversely proportional to the coping energy required to do the job well.

Essentially, coping energy is zero-return energy—that is, it brings you up to zero so you can begin doing the work. If an employee's energy is drained by just coping, there is very little energy left to devote to the job, and performance and job satisfaction suffer as a result. Think of the best job you ever had—one that made you eager to get to work everyday. Chances are you had to expend little, if any, coping energy. Finding a job you love means finding a job that fits with your preferred problem-solving style.

PROBLEM-SOLVING STYLE AND INNOVATION

Figure 6–1 presents a simple problem-solving model placed above the continuum of problem-solving styles.

As this figure indicates, people who prefer to make the system better are naturally gifted at implementation, while people who prefer to make the system different are naturally gifted at generating ideas. By "naturally gifted," we mean that people have natural talents in these particular parts of the innovation process. It would be unrealistic to expect every individual to do well at every part of the innovation process, even though many organizations in the past have expected people "to do the whole job." Today we assemble teams to do the whole job, and by extension, we can assume that an organizational team will be strong to the degree that its members have different problem-solving styles, and each member is working primarily on jobs that require his or her preferred style. Every problem-solving style has a valuable contribution to make to the organization, and everyone has a role to play in the innovation process.

VALUING DIFFERENT PROBLEM-SOLVING STYLES

When groups are asked to list adjectives that describe highly adaptive individuals, they often come up with terms like "stick in the mud," "boring," "dull," and "bean counter." When asked to describe high innovators, they usually offer such terms

Figure 6–1. All styles are needed to solve problems more effectively.

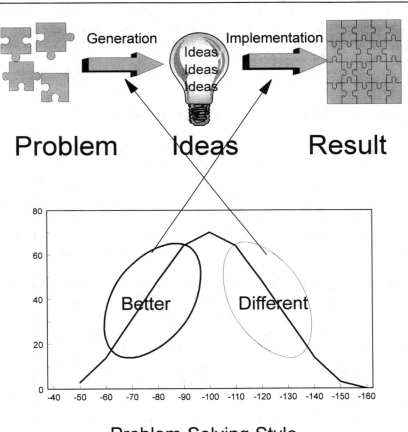

Problem-Solving Style

as "troublemaker," "unfocused," "off the wall," "wacky," and "not serious."

Why do people instantly gravitate to negative descriptions when they are asked about a group different from themselves? We believe it is because humans are herding animals, and the herd defines itself by identifying those outside the herd. It is quite easy to fall into an "us versus them" mentality—people with different nationalities, religions, and ideologies do it all the time. However, for organizational units to become more innovative, employees must change their mindsets, and must truly value those who are different. Consider the fact that when groups are asked to list *valuing* adjectives, they use words like "committed," "accountable," "dependable," and "stable" to describe high adaptors, and "visionary," "pathfinder," "innovative," and "entrepreneur" to describe high innovators.

PROBLEM-SOLVING STYLE AND TEAMWORK

As Figure 6–2 shows, the degree to which team members differ in problem-solving style, and the degree to which different members respect one another, are strongly related to the way that employees behave toward one another and to the effectiveness of the overall team.

For example, think about someone who you believe is close to you on the Adaption/Innovation scale, and someone who you believe is quite far away. Now consider someone you perceive to be quite competent to do his or her job, and someone you perceive to be incompetent. As the upper left quadrant of Figure 6–2 shows, those people you perceive to be competent and similar to you will probably be your friends and, as the upper right quadrant shows, those whom you perceive as competent but quite different are likely to earn your appreciation, because they fill gaps on your team.

By contrast, as the lower left quadrant shows, you are likely to avoid individuals who you perceive as incompetent, but who are very much like you on the Adaption/Innovation scale. You may even view them as "twerps" who take your time but give nothing in return. And finally, as the lower right quadrant shows, you are likely to have strong negative feelings toward those people whom you perceive to be incompetent and also quite different from you. These are the individuals whom you

Figure 6–2. KAI differences and perceived member competence in team member behavior.

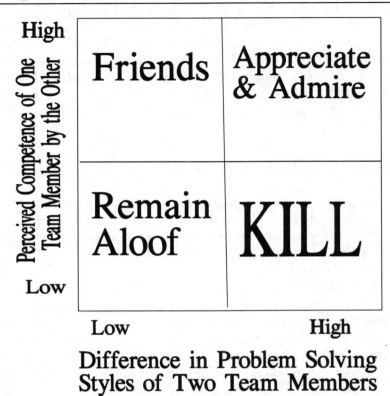

High

Perceived Competence of One
Team Member by the Other

Friends   Appreciate & Admire

Remain Aloof   KILL

Low

Low   High

Difference in Problem Solving
Styles of Two Team Members

figuratively "kill" by undermining them, going around them, or refusing to use their services.

Now that you understand how Figure 6–2 works, how can you help teams function more smoothly in your organization? First, you need to recognize that it's important for teams to include members who place one another in the uppermost quadrants. Obviously it's not always possible to change the people on a team so that its membership is ideal; however, we can improve our *perceptions* of others' competence, by finding a way to make everyone a hero in everyone else's eyes. If you are a team leader, then, one of your primary goals should be to find ways to help your team members recognize and appreciate the contributions of one another. The more they can do this, the more likely that your team will be able to deliver innovative results. In one R&D group at DuPont, the leader asked group members to nominate one member each month for special recognition. The recognition included a description of the individual's contributions and how they helped move the group forward.

NOTE

1. Kirton, M.J., "A Theory of Cognitive Style" in *Adaptors and Innovators, Styles of Creativity and Problem Solving*," Edited by M.J. Kirton (New York: Routledge, New York, 1994).

7

Organizational Structures that Enhance Innovation

No one organizational structure is right for every company. Rather, the structure—that is, the ways in which an organization groups its people, jobs, and responsibilities—must reflect several factors: (1) the company's external environment (the nature of the industry, its degree of competitiveness, etc.); (2) the variations that exist in its markets (e.g., a company operating in a volatile market or with frequent cyclical changes will have a structure that is boundaryless to be successful. Information can enter the company quickly from the outside and be disseminated to appropriate people without being impeded by beauracracy); (3) the firm's unique mix of products, services, and/or processes; (4) the technology the company uses; and (5) management's own structural preferences.

The purpose of an organization's structure is to enable the company to direct and coordinate all of its activities. These activities, often depicted in organizational charts, include:

- The work cycle—who performs each specific type of work, and in what order;

- Communication patterns; and
- Decision-making roles and responsibilities.

The irony about structure, however, is that while it permits the company to organize its tasks and people into a unified whole, these very activities can form a bottleneck *because* of the structure. Structure ideally facilitates innovation by establishing clear paths of communication. But what it can sometimes do is cause units and individuals to become so isolated from one another that change becomes inhibited. Let's look at some examples.

Traditionally, companies structured themselves in ways that emphasized top-down authority relationships, formal patterns of communications, and formal lines of responsibility. Organizations were broken down in segments according to either the type of work performed (for example, employees with similar skills have often been grouped together); the product or market (employees who produce, distribute, or sell the same product or service to the same market have often been grouped together); geography (people in the same region are often grouped in the same office); process (employees work together to move a loan application through approval); or some other similarity (employees who work on the same equipment might be grouped together).

Figure 7–1 depicts a traditional organizational structure that we call the *functional silo*. In this structure, people are grouped into hierarchical units based on the work they perform. Although we call this structure "traditional," it is still very popular, for a few reasons. First, it is among the cheapest of structures to implement, since specific resources can be targeted only to those units where they are needed (i.e., only the R&D department needs the laboratory, only the sales department needs the company cars, and so on). Second, it allows for simple work-distribution decisions: It is easy to determine, for example, who should develop a marketing study (the marketing department) or where a problem involving new wage and

Figure 7–1. The "functional silo" structure that disables innovation.

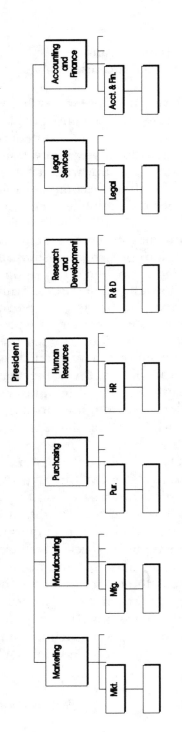

Note Not all positions are shown above. Each functional area has several positions reporting to its director, and many positions at subsequent lower levels.

salary classifications should be solved (the human resources department).

In addition, the functional silo makes it easy to spot where power lies: Decisions in this structure are pushed upward, and made at the top of each functional area, or at the top of the organization itself. Finally, such a structure allows for career development: Newcomers hired at the lowest levels have the opportunity to interact with, report to, and learn from experts with seniority in their specialized fields and in the organization.

However, despite these advantages, the functional silo has several drawbacks that render it less than adequate for the organization that desires to be highly innovative. Its primary weakness (which has led to the "silo" label) is that because individuals are grouped into units based on the type of work they perform, it is unlikely that most members (particularly lower level people who are, of course, closest to the customer and the company's front-line) will interact much with employees outside their unit. Thus, through no fault of their own, these employees will develop a very limited view of the organization and its environment.

Further, people in this type of structure tend to view any problem or issue through their functional "lens," and will probably stick resolutely to their opinions in the face of someone who brings a different function's perspective to the problem. Figure 7–2 humorously (but no less truthfully) illustrates the problems that can occur as a result of the functional silo's failure to promote cross-organizational communication.

Another major flaw of the silo structure is that it slows down change—or, at worst, prevents any change at all. The hierarchical manner in which ideas, information, and decisions must move inhibits action. To obtain approval for something, an individual or department must formulate a request, which must travel up the hierarchy and then down again. Not surprisingly, this process tends to stifle change.

ENABLING STRUCTURES FOR INNOVATION

Alternatively, many structures in use today permit—or even depend on—inter-unit communications as a way of encourag-

Figure 7–2. The name of the game is communications (or lack thereof).

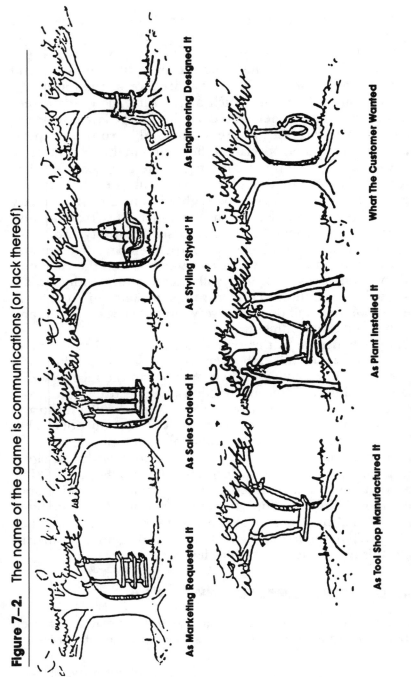

As Marketing Requested It

As Sales Ordered It

As Engineering Designed It

As Styling 'Styled' It

As Tool Shop Manufactured It

As Plant Installed It

What The Customer Wanted

Courtesy of the Tooling and Manufacturing Association

ing innovation. They also often push decisions downward to the lowest levels, so the company can be more responsive to its customers and external environment. These structures tend to have an aesthetic quality: Some are designed to look like wheels, circles, stars, spokes on a bicycle wheel, or other symbols that suggest the absence of hierarchy and formal power relationships.

Another effective structure for innovation is the small team model. In this structure, business units are deliberately kept small in number, and consist of representative members from various functional specialties across the company. For example, an organization might have a team composed of an engineer, a marketer, a financier, a production specialist, and a salesperson. These individuals work together on a project, an approach that enables them to share their varied perspectives. The most important advantage of this structure is that it permits relatively large organizations to move quickly, much like the small businesses with which many are competing today.

Figure 7–3 presents a structure developed by Eastman Chemical Company that enables individuals to be innovative. Eastman calls this structure its "pizza chart." Each of the circles (known as "pepperoni slices") represents a multi-functional team. The proliferation of circles is intended to ensure that top-down thinking and practices are kept to a minimum, while the lines connecting the circles are designed to illustrate that cross-team communication is encouraged.

Eastman's businesses are grouped into market-focused organizations—a clear departure from the traditional product-focused organization. Business and manufacturing organizations interface, and the business organizations actively help manage the overall company.

Finally, you'll notice that there is a bold circular line surrounding the entire organization. This line is intended to illustrate that ongoing communications and networking is expected among all elements of the company. The open space around and between the circles is intended to represent the area in which interaction among teams takes place. This is a

Figure 7–3. The Eastman Chemical pizza.

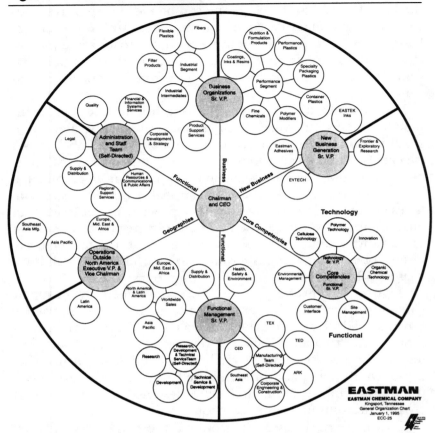

visual representation of open communications which enable employees to work in a matrix organization, unhindered by traditional organizational lines and boundaries.

DESIGNING A STRUCTURE THAT ENCOURAGES INNOVATION

Designing a company structure that enhances, rather than detracts from, its innovative capability may seem like a contradiction in terms. The very attempt to control organizational processes such as communications and knowledge disperse-ment may seem like a good way to stifle, rather than promote, the kind of sharing and spontaneous interactions on which creativity and innovation thrive. However, the enabling organi-zational structures described above will neither restrain nor contain individuals or groups.

Organizations that want to choose a new structure or mod-ify an existing one in an effort to encourage more innovation should study the structures we've described carefully, and should also consider the following guidelines:

• *Begin with a strategy in mind.* Organization leaders should make sure that the firm's purpose or mission directly influences their choice of structure. For example, if the overall purpose of the company (or of a group within the company) is to provide second-to-none service, then its people and jobs should be configured accordingly. This may mean keeping a small group of people with different responsibilities directly in touch with customers. Thus, when the need arises to make a change within the organization, there will be several people who will be very familiar with each customer's particular needs, and how those needs should be met.

• *Arrange for employees to move around the organization.* Employees should spend a short time in various areas other than their own, to get the answers they need, to learn some-thing new, or simply to observe how another group does things. The fancy phrase for this is *boundary spanning.*

• *Consider your company's structure to be flexible, rather than permanent.* Boundaryless organizations may consist of a host of temporary groupings of employees who come together to complete a project and achieve an objective. Once the project is completed, employees disband and join other projects and teams, where they work on something else. Imagine the techni-cal and innovative prowess your company could unleash if employees with specific talents could be assigned temporarily to where they are most needed, regardless of their functional allegiances.

• *Try one of the creativity techniques described in Chapter 4.* Challenging your assumptions about how a company should be designed may lead to unexpected ideas about how a new structure might look. Since structure involves visual, conceptual, and behavioral activities, it is an ideal application for creative-thinking methods.

• *Remember that the contemporary structures that drive innovation are horizontal rather than vertical; dynamic rather than static; and work-driven rather than arbitrarily chosen.* Imagine your organization's structure in a "child-like" way: Allow employees to bend it, stretch it, examine it, and rearrange it to fit up-to-the minute demands. You will find that by loosening your control of the structure, you will end up having more control over what your employees contribute to the overall effectiveness of the group or company.

8

Getting Started on Your Innovation Journey

In this chapter, we present a description of Eastman Chemical Company's "innovation journey," and offer a set of guidelines and questions you can use to help your organization begin or continue its own such journey. First, look at Figure 8–1, which shows how Eastman diagrams its innovation effort. Then, read the company's own description of its effort, as presented in the box on page 84.

To begin your own journey, first assess your organization's innovative position:

• *Where are you now?* What are you currently producing, distributing, and/or selling that could be done a little bit (or quite a bit) better than you are currently doing it?

• *What is right about what you are doing?* (Remember, start with divergent thinking!) How can you improve it to do even better?

• *In what ways might you use processes in this book to help you get there?* Consider which processes might work for specific areas of your organization.

The Innovation Journey:
A Description by Eastman Chemical Company

A lot of people automatically think of Research and Development when they think of innovation. Not Eastman Chemical Company.

Innovation involves all employees from every level and area. That's why innovation is a company process, not an R&D process. And at Eastman, it's driven by the business organizations.

Eastman's Innovation Process begins and ends with the market. It Isn't a sequential, linear process, but one where customer and market needs are considered early in the process, and validated and revalidated throughout the process. That's what the arrows in Eastman's Innovation Process diagram signify—interaction.

The *Needs* part of the process is where the market's need for a product or process is identified, verified, and validated. What do these terms mean?

- *Identification* is discovering a need for which Eastman might add value.
- *Verification* is the process of ensuring shared understanding with the customer.
- *Validation* is the process of determining the relative strategic value of solving the Need to the customer or market and to Eastman.

If these steps are excluded, by the time the project is complete, the customer's need will have undoubtedly changed. History shows this problem is all too common. So the up-front work is very important. At Eastman, a lot of the work of identifying, verifying, and validating a customer need is done in multifunctional Needs Teams established by the business organizations.

After a need is identified, verified, and validated, it needs a solution. That's the *Ideas* stage of the process. This is where creativity plays its most important role and where creative problem solving is used. Eastman has creativity facilitators who are available to help teams problem-solve creatively—until their ideas are exhausted. Ideas are then evaluated until a preferred concept is identified.

The next stage, *Projects,* is where the preferred concept is further defined. This usually involves process scale-up and extensive external sampling to customers. Members from the Ideas Team often serve on this project, which helps provide consistency. Members could be from R&D, engineering, manufacturing, health, safety, environmental, and regulatory legal organizations. Multifunctional teams are very important in every step of Eastman's process.

An Innovation Committee approves and monitors each innovation project, which Eastman calls *Innovation Concepts.* The vice president of the supporting business organization chairs this committee. This approach ensures a common understanding of the project objectives and buy-in from all areas involved in supporting the project. It also works to identify and eliminate barriers.

The final stage is to *Launch* the project. This is where Eastman commercializes the product, develops the market, introduces the product, and develops sales. Market development actually begins early in the life of a project, right from the beginning of identifying a need, but it also plays a major role in the Launch stage. Launch must include understanding who the customers are, what the right way is to deliver a product, and what the right way is to introduce it.

Each stage of the Innovation Process must be in sync with the others. The way to do that is through communication—communication between teams, communication between every level of the company, and communication between the customer and the company. Without constantly communicating with the customer and constantly assessing the needs of the marketplace, a company may think it has solved the problem, when in reality it returns to the customer only to discover everything has changed.

• *Who can you involve in this process?* Force yourself out of the zones of comfort in which you have been operating, and think about including individuals and groups who have not been included previously: employees from lower levels, customers, suppliers/vendors, members of the business community, and even selected competitors (that is, competitors who may be concerned about the same problems, but may not be serving the same market segments or customer groups). Include others during idea generation who may be able to contribute a fresh perspective on your situation.

Figure 8–1. How Eastman Chemical diagrams innovation.

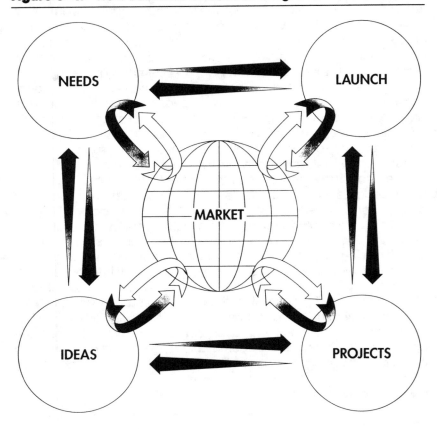

• *How can you help other individuals and groups whose acceptance is needed to join in the journey?* To give your innovation initiative credibility, it's important to demonstrate quickly that the effort has business value, and to bring "nay-sayers" on board. Start with an important problem for which there are no easy or obvious solutions. Ask a senior executive to let you use your approach during his or her next problem meeting. Assemble a core group whose job it is to solve the problem, and include the senior executive on the team (if the executive will not take the time, the problem isn't important enough). Use an experienced facilitator to guide your group through a focused workshop to generate new, useful, and unexpected ideas. Ensure that action is taken on the best ideas, and ensure that progress is communicated to all the participants.

We recommend that you not use power, forcing people to participate: The risk is that you will have people who are physically present but cognitively absent. If people are not personally committed, they will simply not contribute all that they can, and time and energy will be wasted. Instead, create a situation in which people will want to participate. You need to help them realize that the benefits (e.g., profitability, a rise in market share, winning a new account, or such personal accomplishments as career development) will clearly outweigh the costs.

• *What should you work on improving first?* We recommend that you take a good, hard look at your working environment. Select two or three of the dimensions listed in Chapter 5 that you believe are hindering innovation, assemble a team to tackle them one by one, and take purposeful action.

MORE QUESTIONS TO ASK YOURSELF

In previous chapters, we saw that even well-meaning, highly creative, determined individuals will have an arduous uphill climb if they must constantly fight against a prohibitive company culture. Identifying barriers to creativity and innovation before you start your journey will help you focus your efforts and ensure improvements. Here are some additional questions to ask yourself:

• *How clear is top management about the purpose and mission of the business?* The company's vision itself should be well articulated and well understood, and the interpretation of the vision by each organizational unit should be accurate. Each unit should also be aware of the other units' roles. It is easy to see that a horizontal structure will help ensure such company-wide comprehension: When employees and teams have the opportunity to communicate with one another frequently, the chance that anyone will misunderstand or fantasize about what "they" are up to now is greatly reduced.

• *What are your team and company norms? What are people expected to do?* To identify these norms, consider asking some of your relatively new hires about their perceptions upon joining the team or organization. Who do they believe fits in or gets ahead in the company? Who do they think are the heroes and the villains? To modify or change the culture for innovation, you must first diagnose what the "old" norms are.

• *What does your organization expect from its improvement process?* Are these expectations realistic? Often innovative efforts fail not because the idea lacks merit, but because the implementation did not go quite as planned and the return was less than anticipated. When this has happened, we have seen many companies scrap the plan, lose all that had been invested until that point, and develop a "learned helplessness" attitude towards innovation and change.

• *What are the organizational barriers to innovation?* What levels of bureaucracy have we accepted that we can eliminate?

SETTING OFF ON THE JOURNEY

As any product-development professional will tell you, most successful new products or services do not provide adequate returns until the second or third stages of development. The same is true of any innovation initiative. Thus, it's important to set an organization mindset of "sticking with it through the long haul."

Remember that starting an innovation effort is like filling the Alaska Pipeline: Once you've started the process, it will take a while before you can recognize that you've made any appreciable strides, because the pipeline is long and the time delay is significant. You must give the process time. If you are reasonably sure that your organization is doing the right things, innovation will occur in due time.

Appendix:

Nine Workplace Dimensions that Support Creativity and Innovation

1. Challenge and Involvement

Description:

This dimension refers to the degree to which people are involved in daily operations, long-term goals, and visions. A high level of challenge and involvement means that people are intrinsically motivated and committed to making contributions to the organization. It also means that the climate has a dynamic, electric, and inspiring quality, and that people find joy and meaningfulness in their work, so they invest much energy. In the opposite situation, people are not engaged, and feelings of alienation and indifference are present. In addition, employees commonly feel apathetic, they lack interest in their work, and they are dull and listless in their interactions.

A Question for Managers to Ask Themselves:

Do people here feel deeply committed to their jobs?

2. Freedom

Description:

This dimension refers to the degree of independent behavior that people in the organization demonstrate. In a climate with much freedom, people are given the autonomy to define much of their own work. They can exercise discretion in their day-to-day activities, and they take the initiative to acquire and share information, and to make plans and decisions about their work. In the opposite climate, people confront strict guidelines and roles. They carry out their work in prescribed ways, and have little opportunity to redefine their tasks.

A Question for Managers to Ask Themselves:

Do most people here usually control their own work?

3. Idea Time

Description:

This dimension refers to the amount of time people can use (and do use) for elaborating on new ideas. In a high idea-time situation, employees have the chance to discuss and test impulses and fresh approaches. In the reverse case, every minute is booked and specified, and time pressure makes thinking about anything other than the planned routines impossible.

A Question for Managers to Ask Themselves:

Do people here have the time to consider alternatives?

4. Idea Support

Description:

This dimension refers to the way in which new ideas are treated. In a supportive climate, bosses, peers, and subordinates all receive ideas and suggestions in an attentive and professional way. People listen to one another, encourage initiatives, and create possibilities for trying out new ideas. The atmosphere surrounding new ideas is constructive and positive. When idea support is low, an automatic "no" prevails. Eery suggestion is immediately refuted by a destructive counter-argument. People typically respond to new ideas by finding faults and raising obstacles.

A Question for Managers to Ask Themselves:

Do people generally share their ideas here, confident that they will be listened to and encouraged?

5. Conflict

Description:

This dimension refers to the level of personal and emotional tension (as opposed to intellectual, stimulating tension) that exists in the organization. When the level of conflict is high, individuals and groups dislike—or may even hate—one another. "Interpersonal warfare" proliferates: Plots, traps, gossip, slander, and power and territory struggles are part of everyday life. In the opposite case, people behave in a more mature manner. They control their negative impulses, and they accept and deal effectively with diversity.

A Question for Managers to Ask Themselves:

Is there a great deal of personal tension here?

6. Debates

Description:

This dimension refers to the encounters and disagreements that take place in which employees express different viewpoints, ideas, experiences, and knowledge. In an organization that engages in debates, many voices are heard, and people are keen on putting forward their ideas for consideration and review. People can often be seen discussing opposing opinions and diverse perspectives. When debates are missing, people follow authoritarian patterns without questioning them.

A Question for Managers to Ask Themselves:

Is a diversity of perspectives allowed here?

7. Playfulness and Humor

Description:

This dimension refers to the level of spontaneity and ease displayed in the workplace. A relaxed atmosphere where good-natured jokes and laughter are heard often reflects a high playfulness/humor environment. People can be seen having fun, and the atmosphere is perceived as easygoing and light-hearted. The opposite climate is characterized by gravity and seriousness. The atmosphere is stiff, gloomy, and oppressive. Jokes and laughter are regarded as improper and intolerable.

A Question for Managers to Ask Themselves:

Do good-natured joking and teasing occur frequently here?

8. Trust and Openness

Description:

This dimension refers to the emotional safety found in the workplace's relationships. When there is trust, individuals can be open and frank with one another. People can count on each other for personal support, and they have a sincere respect for one another. When trust is missing, people are suspicious of one another. Therefore, they closely guard themselves and their ideas. In such situations, people find it extremely difficult to communicate openly with each other.

Do people here talk behind each others' backs?

9. Risk-Taking

Description:

This dimension refers to the degree to which uncertainty and ambiguity are tolerated in the workplace. In a high risk-taking environment, employees will take bold new initiatives, even if the outcomes are unknown. People feel as though they can "take a gamble" on some of their ideas, and they will often "go out on a limb" and be first to put an idea forward. In a risk-avoiding climate, by contrast, employees have a cautious, hesitant mentality. People try to be on the "safe side" and often decide "to sleep on the matter" rather than giving their ideas a shot. They set up committees and cover themselves in many ways before making a decision.

A Question for Managers to Ask Themselves:

Do people here feel they can take bold action even if the expected outcome is unclear?

Adapted from: Isaksen, S.G., Dorval, K.B., and Treffinger, D.J., *Creative Approaches to Problem Solving* (Dubuque, Iowa: Kendall/ Hunt Publishing Company, 1994).

About the Authors

Charles W. Prather earned his Ph.D. in biochemistry from North Carolina State University. He joined DuPont as a research chemist and served for 18 years in numerous R&D management positions. Charlie was appointed manager of the DuPont Center for Creativity & Innovation upon its formation and helped shape its direction and design its offerings. Today, he helps organizations apply the principles of innovation with his workshop series, "Bottom Line Innovation."

Lisa Gundry is associate professor of management in the Charles H. Kellstadt Graduate School of Business at DePaul University, where she teaches courses in entrepreneurship, organizational behavior, and creativity in organizations. Prior to joining DePaul, she was a research analyst for a private sector research institute and a health care organization. She has written for a number of journals, including *Human Relations, IEEE Transactions on Engineering Management,* and *Organizational Dynamics.* She consults with organizations on issues such as small business development and managing change. She received her Ph.D. from Northwestern University.

For additional copies of **Blueprints for Innovation: How Creative Processes Can Make You and Your Company More Competitive** . . .

CALL: **1-800-262-9699**
1-518-891-1500 (outside the U.S.)

FAX: **1-518-891-0368**

WRITE: **Management Briefings**
AMA Publication Services
P.O. Box 319
Saranac Lake, NY 12983

Ask for **Stock #02359XMFB.** $14.95 per single copy/AMA Members $13.45. Discounts for bulk orders (5 or more copies).

OTHER AMA PUBLICATIONS OF INTEREST

The Management Compass: Steering the Corporation Using Hoshin Planning

Examines the fundamentals of *hoshin planning,* a strategic management methodology originated in Japan, that is gaining rapid acceptance with U.S. companies. Stock #02358XMB, $19.95/$17.95 AMA Members.

Mentoring: Helping Employees Reach Their Full Potential

Explains how mentoring has progressed to an information-age model of helping people learn and offers opportunities for organizational rejuvenation, competitive adaptation, and employee development. Stock #02357XMFB, $14.95/$13.45 AMA Members.

Blueprints for Service Quality: The Federal Express Approach, SECOND EDITION

Detailed, how-to information on personnel practices and quality measurement systems at Federal Express. Recently updated. Stock #02356XMFB, $12.50/$11.25 AMA Members.

Quality Alone Is Not Enough

Puts quality improvement programs into perspective, and provides tools for measuring quality, linking time and quality, and achieving the shortest path to quality. Stock #02349XMFB, $12.95/$11.65 AMA Members.

The Creative Edge: How Companies Support Creativity and Innovation

Learn how company policies, training programs, and strategic planning sharpen creativity and innovation and continue to drive the competitive edge toward business success. Also learn why "creative imitation" is sometimes better than creative innovation. Stock #06712XMFB, $29.95/$26.95 AMA Members.

Complete the ORDER FORM on the following page. For faster service, **CALL** or **FAX** your order.

PERIODICALS ORDER FORM
(Discounts for bulk orders of five or more copies.)

Please send me the following:

☐ ＿＿ copies of **Blueprints for Innovation: How Creative Processes Can Make You and Your Company More Competitive,** Stock #02359XMFB, $14.95/$13.45 AMA Members.

☐ ＿＿ copies of **The Management Compass: Steering the Corporation Using Hoshin Planning.** Stock #02358XMFB, $19.95/$17.95 AMA Members.

☐ ＿＿ copies of **Mentoring: Helping Employees Reach Their Full Potential,** Stock #02357XMFB, $14.95/$13.45 AMA Members.

☐ ＿＿ copies of **Blueprints for Service Quality: The Federal Express Approach, SECOND EDITION,** Stock #02356XMFB, $12.50/$11.25 AMA Members.

☐ ＿＿ copies of **Quality Alone Is Not Enough,** Stock #02349XMFB, $12.95/$11.65 AMA Members.

☐ ＿＿ copies of **The Creative Edge: How Companies Support Creativity and Innovation,** Stock #06712XMFB, $29.95/$26.95 AMA Members.

Name: ＿＿＿＿＿＿＿＿＿＿＿＿＿＿＿＿＿＿＿＿＿＿

Title: ＿＿＿＿＿＿＿＿＿＿＿＿＿＿＿＿＿＿＿＿＿＿＿

Organization: ＿＿＿＿＿＿＿＿＿＿＿＿＿＿＿＿＿＿＿

Street Address: ＿＿＿＿＿＿＿＿＿＿＿＿＿＿＿＿＿＿

City, State, Zip: ＿＿＿＿＿＿＿＿＿＿＿＿＿＿＿＿＿＿

Phone: (   ) ＿＿＿＿＿＿＿＿＿＿＿＿＿＿＿＿＿＿

Sales tax, if applicable, and shipping & handling will be added.

☐ Charge my credit card.　　☐ Bill me.
☐ Bill my company.　　☐ AMA Member.

Card #: ＿ ＿ ＿ ＿ ＿ ＿ ＿ ＿ ＿ ＿ ＿ ＿ ＿ ＿ ＿ ＿　Exp. Date ＿＿＿＿＿＿

Signature: ＿＿＿＿＿＿＿＿＿＿＿＿＿＿＿＿＿＿＿＿＿

Purchase Order #: ＿＿＿＿＿＿＿＿＿＿＿＿＿＿＿＿＿

AMA'S NO-RISK GUARANTEE: If for any reason you are not satisfied, we will credit the purchase price toward another product or refund your money. **No hassles. No loopholes. Just excellent service. That is what AMA is all about.**

AMA Publication Services
P.O. Box 319
Saranac Lake, NY 12983